# TEACHER'S PET PUBLICATIONS

## PUZZLE PACK
for
Narrative of the Life of Frederick Douglass

based on the autobiography by
Frederick Douglass

Written by
Mary B. Collins

© 2008 Teacher's Pet Publications
All Rights Reserved

The materials in this packet are copyrighted
by Teacher's Pet Publications, Inc.

These pages may be duplicated by the purchaser
for use in the purchaser's own classroom.

Copying any of these materials and distributing them
for any other purpose is a violation of the copyright laws.

© 2008 Teacher's Pet Publications, Inc.
www.tpet.com

## INTRODUCTION
If you already own the LitPlan for this title, this Puzzle Pack will refresh your Unit Resource Materials and Vocabulary Resource Materials sections plus give you additional materials you can substitute into the tests. If you do not already have a complete LitPlan, these pages will give you some supplemental materials to use with your own plan. There are two main groups of materials: one set for unit words (such as characters' names, symbols, places, etc.) and one set for vocabulary words associated with the book.

## WORD LIST
There is a word list for both the unit words and the vocabulary words. These lists show you which words are being used in the materials and the clues or definitions being used for those words. You may want to give students a word list with clues/definitions to help them, or you may want students to only have a word list (without clues/definitions) if you want them to work a little harder. Both are available for duplication. The word lists can also be your "calling key" for the bingo games.

## FILL IN THE BLANK AND MATCHING
There are 4 each of the fill in the blank and matching worksheets for both the unit and vocabulary words. These pages can be used either as extra worksheets for students or as objective parts of a unit test. They can be done individually if students need extra help or as a whole class activity to review the material covered.

## MAGIC SQUARES
The magic squares not only reinforce the material covered but also work on reasoning and math skills. Many teachers have told us that their students really enjoy doing these!

## WORD SEARCH PUZZLES
The word search words go in all directions, as indicated on your answer keys. Two of the word search puzzles have the clues listed rather than the words. This makes the puzzle a little more difficult, but it reinforces the material better. Two word search puzzles have words only for students who find the clue puzzles too difficult.

## CROSSWORD PUZZLES
Both unit and vocabulary word sections have 4 crossword puzzles.

## BINGO CARDS
There are 32 individual bingo cards for the unit words and 32 individual bingo cards for the vocabulary words. You can use your word list as a "call list," calling the words at random and marking them off of your list as you go, or you could use the flash cards by cutting them apart and drawing the words at random from a hat (or box or whatever). To make a better review, you might ask for the definition and spelling of each word as you call it out–or you could call out the definitions and have students tell you the words they need to look for on the puzzle.

## JUGGLE LETTERS
The vocabulary juggle letter game is intended to help students learn the spellings of the words. One sheet has the definitions listed on it as an extra help for students who need it or to reinforce the definitions if you choose to do so.

## FLASH CARDS
We've included a set of vocabulary flash cards you can duplicate, cut, and fold for your students. Some teachers make a few sets for general use by the class; others make a set for each student. Some teachers duplicate them for each student and have the students cut & fold their own. You can cut out just the words and put them in a hat, have each student pick out one word and write the definition and a sentence for that word. Students then swap words and papers, with the next student adding a sentence of his own under the last one. You can have students swap as many times as you like. Each time the student will read the sentences written prior to his own and then add a sentence. You can cut out the words and definitions separately and play "I Have; Who Has?" Each student in the room draws a word and definition. The first student says, "I have (the name of the word). Who has the definition?" The student with the definition reads it then says, "I have (the name of the vocabulary word she has). Who has the definition?" The round continues until all words and definitions have been given.

## Frederick Douglass Word List

| No. | Word | Clue/Definition |
|---|---|---|
| 1. | ABOLITIONISTS | Douglass learned about these anti-slavery people from the newspaper |
| 2. | ANNA | Douglass's wife |
| 3. | ANTHONY | Douglass's white father, clerk to Lloyd: Aaron ___ |
| 4. | ARTFUL | Douglass described Mr. Gore as cruel, ___, and obdurate. |
| 5. | AULD | Taught Douglass some of the alphabet and spelling |
| 6. | BAILEY | Douglass's last name at birth |
| 7. | BALTIMORE | Douglass lived there with Hugh Auld. |
| 8. | BEAL | Shot and killed a slave with a musket: ___ Bondy |
| 9. | BEDFORD | Douglass moved here from New York: New ___ |
| 10. | BIRTH | 1818 is the estimated year of Douglass's ___. |
| 11. | BREAD | Douglass traded it for reading lessons from white boys. |
| 12. | CAULKING | Douglass's learned trade, done to ships |
| 13. | COLUMBIAN | Reading The ___ Orator helped Douglass argue against slavery. |
| 14. | COVEY | Slave breaker Douglass eventually beat |
| 15. | DANIEL | Lloyd who protected Frederick from older boys |
| 16. | DEMBY | Shot by Gore |
| 17. | DEVIL | Served by the slaveholding religion |
| 18. | DOUGLASS | Name came from the book Lady of the Lake |
| 19. | ESCAPE | This was easier to do from the city. |
| 20. | FREDERICK | He escaped slavery and became a great orator. |
| 21. | GOD | Douglass attributed his good fortune to ___. |
| 22. | GORE | Cruel; gave severe punishments |
| 23. | GRANDMOTHER | She raised Frederick after he was taken from his mother. |
| 24. | HAM | Was cursed in the Bible; slaves supposedly descended from him |
| 25. | HARRIET | Douglass's mother |
| 26. | HICK | Murdered Douglass's wife's cousin |
| 27. | HIRING | Douglass considered it as a step towards freedom: ___ out |
| 28. | JENKINS | Slave who gave Douglass the root |
| 29. | JOHNSON | Last name Douglass used in New York |
| 30. | LANMAN | Killed two slaves, one with a hatchet |
| 31. | LIBERATOR | Paper Douglass began reading in New York |
| 32. | LLOYD | Col. who owned the plantation where Douglass first lived |
| 33. | MULATTO | Child with slave mother and white father |
| 34. | NANTUCKET | Location of anti-slavery meeting where Douglass first spoke |
| 35. | RELIGIOUS | Slaveholders of the worst kind had this quality. |
| 36. | ROOT | Supposed to keep slaves from being whipped: lucky ___ |
| 37. | RUGGLES | David who helped Douglass in New York |
| 38. | SEPTEMBER | Month of Douglass's final escape |
| 39. | SEVEN | Douglass's age when his mother died |
| 40. | SHIPYARD | Douglass worked here when he learned to write. |
| 41. | SINGING | Done when slaves were unhappy, not happy as believed |
| 42. | SIX | Number of cents Hugh Auld gave Douglass from his wages |
| 43. | TAR | The Colonel used it to keep slaves out of the garden. |
| 44. | THOMAS | Did not give slaves enough to eat: Master ___ |
| 45. | TIMBER | Douglass copied letters on it to learn to write. |
| 46. | TUCKAHOE | Douglass's birthplace |

Frederick Douglass Fill In The Blanks 1

_____

_____

_____

_____

_____

_____

_____

_____

_____

_____

_____

_____

_____

_____

_____

_____

_____

_____

_____

_____

1. Lloyd who protected Frederick from older boys
2. Cruel; gave severe punishments
3. Douglass's learned trade, done to ships
4. Col. who owned the plantation where Douglass first lived
5. 1818 is the estimated year of Douglass's ___.
6. She raised Frederick after he was taken from his mother.
7. Douglass described Mr. Gore as cruel, ___, and obdurate.
8. Douglass learned about these anti-slavery people from the newspaper
9. Month of Douglass's final escape
10. Killed two slaves, one with a hatchet
11. Shot by Gore
12. The Colonel used it to keep slaves out of the garden.
13. Last name Douglass used in New York
14. Douglass's white father, clerk to Lloyd: Aaron ___
15. Child with slave mother and white father
16. Supposed to keep slaves from being whipped: lucky ___
17. Douglass moved here from New York: New ___
18. Douglass's age when his mother died
19. He escaped slavery and became a great orator.
20. This was easier to do from the city.

Frederick Douglass Fill In The Blanks 1 Answer Key

|  |  |
|---|---|
| DANIEL | 1. Lloyd who protected Frederick from older boys |
| GORE | 2. Cruel; gave severe punishments |
| CAULKING | 3. Douglass's learned trade, done to ships |
| LLOYD | 4. Col. who owned the plantation where Douglass first lived |
| BIRTH | 5. 1818 is the estimated year of Douglass's ___. |
| GRANDMOTHER | 6. She raised Frederick after he was taken from his mother. |
| ARTFUL | 7. Douglass described Mr. Gore as cruel, ___, and obdurate. |
| ABOLITIONISTS | 8. Douglass learned about these anti-slavery people from the newspaper |
| SEPTEMBER | 9. Month of Douglass's final escape |
| LANMAN | 10. Killed two slaves, one with a hatchet |
| DEMBY | 11. Shot by Gore |
| TAR | 12. The Colonel used it to keep slaves out of the garden. |
| JOHNSON | 13. Last name Douglass used in New York |
| ANTHONY | 14. Douglass's white father, clerk to Lloyd: Aaron ___ |
| MULATTO | 15. Child with slave mother and white father |
| ROOT | 16. Supposed to keep slaves from being whipped: lucky ___ |
| BEDFORD | 17. Douglass moved here from New York: New ___ |
| SEVEN | 18. Douglass's age when his mother died |
| FREDERICK | 19. He escaped slavery and became a great orator. |
| ESCAPE | 20. This was easier to do from the city. |

Frederick Douglass Fill In The Blanks 2

1. He escaped slavery and became a great orator.
2. Name came from the book Lady of the Lake
3. She raised Frederick after he was taken from his mother.
4. Douglass's learned trade, done to ships
5. Shot by Gore
6. Douglass's birthplace
7. Lloyd who protected Frederick from older boys
8. Served by the slaveholding religion
9. Reading The ___ Orator helped Douglass argue against slavery.
10. Douglass copied letters on it to learn to write.
11. Douglass moved here from New York: New ___
12. Douglass worked here when he learned to write.
13. Did not give slaves enough to eat: Master ___
14. Douglass described Mr. Gore as cruel, ___, and obdurate.
15. Supposed to keep slaves from being whipped: lucky ___
16. Col. who owned the plantation where Douglass first lived
17. Slaveholders of the worst kind had this quality.
18. Douglass considered it as a step towards freedom: ___ out
19. Done when slaves were unhappy, not happy as believed
20. Child with slave mother and white father

Frederick Douglass Fill In The Blanks 2 Answer Key

| | |
|---|---|
| FREDERICK | 1. He escaped slavery and became a great orator. |
| DOUGLASS | 2. Name came from the book Lady of the Lake |
| GRANDMOTHER | 3. She raised Frederick after he was taken from his mother. |
| CAULKING | 4. Douglass's learned trade, done to ships |
| DEMBY | 5. Shot by Gore |
| TUCKAHOE | 6. Douglass's birthplace |
| DANIEL | 7. Lloyd who protected Frederick from older boys |
| DEVIL | 8. Served by the slaveholding religion |
| COLUMBIAN | 9. Reading The ___ Orator helped Douglass argue against slavery. |
| TIMBER | 10. Douglass copied letters on it to learn to write. |
| BEDFORD | 11. Douglass moved here from New York: New ___ |
| SHIPYARD | 12. Douglass worked here when he learned to write. |
| THOMAS | 13. Did not give slaves enough to eat: Master ___ |
| ARTFUL | 14. Douglass described Mr. Gore as cruel, ___, and obdurate. |
| ROOT | 15. Supposed to keep slaves from being whipped: lucky ___ |
| LLOYD | 16. Col. who owned the plantation where Douglass first lived |
| RELIGIOUS | 17. Slaveholders of the worst kind had this quality. |
| HIRING | 18. Douglass considered it as a step towards freedom: ___ out |
| SINGING | 19. Done when slaves were unhappy, not happy as believed |
| MULATTO | 20. Child with slave mother and white father |

Frederick Douglass Fill In The Blanks 3

_____

_____

_____

_____

_____

_____

_____

_____

_____

_____

_____

_____

_____

_____

_____

_____

_____

_____

_____

_____

1. She raised Frederick after he was taken from his mother.
2. The Colonel used it to keep slaves out of the garden.
3. This was easier to do from the city.
4. Taught Douglass some of the alphabet and spelling
5. Douglass's age when his mother died
6. Douglass's mother
7. Douglass lived there with Hugh Auld.
8. Reading The ___ Orator helped Douglass argue against slavery.
9. Shot by Gore
10. Douglass copied letters on it to learn to write.
11. Douglass moved here from New York: New ___
12. 1818 is the estimated year of Douglass's ___.
13. Supposed to keep slaves from being whipped: lucky ___
14. Cruel; gave severe punishments
15. Slave breaker Douglass eventually beat
16. Last name Douglass used in New York
17. Douglass's white father, clerk to Lloyd: Aaron ___
18. Douglass considered it as a step towards freedom: ___ out
19. Location of anti-slavery meeting where Douglass first spoke
20. Douglass attributed his good fortune to ___.

Frederick Douglass Fill In The Blanks 3 Answer Key

| | |
|---|---|
| GRANDMOTHER | 1. She raised Frederick after he was taken from his mother. |
| TAR | 2. The Colonel used it to keep slaves out of the garden. |
| ESCAPE | 3. This was easier to do from the city. |
| AULD | 4. Taught Douglass some of the alphabet and spelling |
| SEVEN | 5. Douglass's age when his mother died |
| HARRIET | 6. Douglass's mother |
| BALTIMORE | 7. Douglass lived there with Hugh Auld. |
| COLUMBIAN | 8. Reading The ___ Orator helped Douglass argue against slavery. |
| DEMBY | 9. Shot by Gore |
| TIMBER | 10. Douglass copied letters on it to learn to write. |
| BEDFORD | 11. Douglass moved here from New York: New ___ |
| BIRTH | 12. 1818 is the estimated year of Douglass's ___. |
| ROOT | 13. Supposed to keep slaves from being whipped: lucky ___ |
| GORE | 14. Cruel; gave severe punishments |
| COVEY | 15. Slave breaker Douglass eventually beat |
| JOHNSON | 16. Last name Douglass used in New York |
| ANTHONY | 17. Douglass's white father, clerk to Lloyd: Aaron ___ |
| HIRING | 18. Douglass considered it as a step towards freedom: ___ out |
| NANTUCKET | 19. Location of anti-slavery meeting where Douglass first spoke |
| GOD | 20. Douglass attributed his good fortune to ___. |

Frederick Douglass Fill In The Blanks 4

1. Month of Douglass's final escape
2. Douglass attributed his good fortune to ___.
3. Douglass traded it for reading lessons from white boys.
4. Douglass learned about these anti-slavery people from the newspaper
5. Douglass's birthplace
6. He escaped slavery and became a great orator.
7. Killed two slaves, one with a hatchet
8. She raised Frederick after he was taken from his mother.
9. Paper Douglass began reading in New York
10. Taught Douglass some of the alphabet and spelling
11. Slave who gave Douglass the root
12. Slave breaker Douglass eventually beat
13. Douglass described Mr. Gore as cruel, ___, and obdurate.
14. Child with slave mother and white father
15. Douglass's mother
16. Douglass lived there with Hugh Auld.
17. The Colonel used it to keep slaves out of the garden.
18. Douglass's age when his mother died
19. Number of cents Hugh Auld gave Douglass from his wages
20. Cruel; gave severe punishments

Frederick Douglass Fill In The Blanks 4 Answer Key

| | |
|---|---|
| SEPTEMBER | 1. Month of Douglass's final escape |
| GOD | 2. Douglass attributed his good fortune to ___. |
| BREAD | 3. Douglass traded it for reading lessons from white boys. |
| ABOLITIONISTS | 4. Douglass learned about these anti-slavery people from the newspaper |
| TUCKAHOE | 5. Douglass's birthplace |
| FREDERICK | 6. He escaped slavery and became a great orator. |
| LANMAN | 7. Killed two slaves, one with a hatchet |
| GRANDMOTHER | 8. She raised Frederick after he was taken from his mother. |
| LIBERATOR | 9. Paper Douglass began reading in New York |
| AULD | 10. Taught Douglass some of the alphabet and spelling |
| JENKINS | 11. Slave who gave Douglass the root |
| COVEY | 12. Slave breaker Douglass eventually beat |
| ARTFUL | 13. Douglass described Mr. Gore as cruel, ___, and obdurate. |
| MULATTO | 14. Child with slave mother and white father |
| HARRIET | 15. Douglass's mother |
| BALTIMORE | 16. Douglass lived there with Hugh Auld. |
| TAR | 17. The Colonel used it to keep slaves out of the garden. |
| SEVEN | 18. Douglass's age when his mother died |
| SIX | 19. Number of cents Hugh Auld gave Douglass from his wages |
| GORE | 20. Cruel; gave severe punishments |

Frederick Douglass Matching 1

___ 1. JOHNSON  
___ 2. DEMBY  
___ 3. LLOYD  
___ 4. BEAL  
___ 5. ANTHONY  
___ 6. HIRING  
___ 7. BIRTH  
___ 8. LANMAN  
___ 9. RUGGLES  
___10. GORE  
___11. BEDFORD  
___12. GRANDMOTHER  
___13. CAULKING  
___14. ARTFUL  
___15. SEVEN  
___16. COVEY  
___17. TIMBER  
___18. HICK  
___19. HAM  
___20. BREAD  
___21. HARRIET  
___22. ROOT  
___23. DANIEL  
___24. SHIPYARD  
___25. ANNA  

A. Shot by Gore  
B. Douglass copied letters on it to learn to write.  
C. Douglass considered it as a step towards freedom: ___ out  
D. Killed two slaves, one with a hatchet  
E. Lloyd who protected Frederick from older boys  
F. Cruel; gave severe punishments  
G. David who helped Douglass in New York  
H. Slave breaker Douglass eventually beat  
I. Supposed to keep slaves from being whipped: lucky ___  
J. Murdered Douglass's wife's cousin  
K. Douglass's mother  
L. Douglass's white father, clerk to Lloyd: Aaron ___  
M. Douglass moved here from New York: New ___  
N. Col. who owned the plantation where Douglass first lived  
O. Douglass described Mr. Gore as cruel, ___, and obdurate.  
P. Douglass worked here when he learned to write.  
Q. Douglass's age when his mother died  
R. Last name Douglass used in New York  
S. Douglass's learned trade, done to ships  
T. Douglass traded it for reading lessons from white boys.  
U. Shot and killed a slave with a musket: ___ Bondy  
V. Douglass's wife  
W. She raised Frederick after he was taken from his mother.  
X. 1818 is the estimated year of Douglass's ___.  
Y. Was cursed in the Bible; slaves supposedly descended from him

Frederick Douglass Matching 1 Answer Key

| | |
|---|---|
| R - 1. JOHNSON | A. Shot by Gore |
| A - 2. DEMBY | B. Douglass copied letters on it to learn to write. |
| N - 3. LLOYD | C. Douglass considered it as a step towards freedom: ___ out |
| U - 4. BEAL | D. Killed two slaves, one with a hatchet |
| L - 5. ANTHONY | E. Lloyd who protected Frederick from older boys |
| C - 6. HIRING | F. Cruel; gave severe punishments |
| X - 7. BIRTH | G. David who helped Douglass in New York |
| D - 8. LANMAN | H. Slave breaker Douglass eventually beat |
| G - 9. RUGGLES | I. Supposed to keep slaves from being whipped: lucky ___ |
| F - 10. GORE | J. Murdered Douglass's wife's cousin |
| M - 11. BEDFORD | K. Douglass's mother |
| W - 12. GRANDMOTHER | L. Douglass's white father, clerk to Lloyd: Aaron ___ |
| S - 13. CAULKING | M. Douglass moved here from New York: New ___ |
| O - 14. ARTFUL | N. Col. who owned the plantation where Douglass first lived |
| Q - 15. SEVEN | O. Douglass described Mr. Gore as cruel, ___, and obdurate. |
| H - 16. COVEY | P. Douglass worked here when he learned to write. |
| B - 17. TIMBER | Q. Douglass's age when his mother died |
| J - 18. HICK | R. Last name Douglass used in New York |
| Y - 19. HAM | S. Douglass's learned trade, done to ships |
| T - 20. BREAD | T. Douglass traded it for reading lessons from white boys. |
| K - 21. HARRIET | U. Shot and killed a slave with a musket: ___ Bondy |
| I - 22. ROOT | V. Douglass's wife |
| E - 23. DANIEL | W. She raised Frederick after he was taken from his mother. |
| P - 24. SHIPYARD | X. 1818 is the estimated year of Douglass's ___. |
| V - 25. ANNA | Y. Was cursed in the Bible; slaves supposedly descended from him |

Frederick Douglass Matching 2

___ 1. SINGING
___ 2. BAILEY
___ 3. TIMBER
___ 4. CAULKING
___ 5. HIRING
___ 6. AULD
___ 7. GORE
___ 8. HAM
___ 9. ANNA
___ 10. MULATTO
___ 11. FREDERICK
___ 12. SHIPYARD
___ 13. ROOT
___ 14. ESCAPE
___ 15. SEPTEMBER
___ 16. TUCKAHOE
___ 17. JENKINS
___ 18. GOD
___ 19. HICK
___ 20. ANTHONY
___ 21. RUGGLES
___ 22. TAR
___ 23. NANTUCKET
___ 24. SEVEN
___ 25. DEVIL

A. Douglass's birthplace
B. Taught Douglass some of the alphabet and spelling
C. Douglass's white father, clerk to Lloyd: Aaron ___
D. He escaped slavery and became a great orator.
E. Douglass's last name at birth
F. Douglass attributed his good fortune to ___.
G. Was cursed in the Bible; slaves supposedly descended from him
H. Douglass worked here when he learned to write.
I. Month of Douglass's final escape
J. Douglass's wife
K. The Colonel used it to keep slaves out of the garden.
L. Served by the slaveholding religion
M. Done when slaves were unhappy, not happy as believed
N. Slave who gave Douglass the root
O. Child with slave mother and white father
P. Douglass's age when his mother died
Q. David who helped Douglass in New York
R. Location of anti-slavery meeting where Douglass first spoke
S. Douglass considered it as a step towards freedom: ___ out
T. This was easier to do from the city.
U. Supposed to keep slaves from being whipped: lucky ___
V. Douglass's learned trade, done to ships
W. Douglass copied letters on it to learn to write.
X. Murdered Douglass's wife's cousin
Y. Cruel; gave severe punishments

Frederick Douglass Matching 2 Answer Key

| | |
|---|---|
| M - 1. SINGING | A. Douglass's birthplace |
| E - 2. BAILEY | B. Taught Douglass some of the alphabet and spelling |
| W - 3. TIMBER | C. Douglass's white father, clerk to Lloyd: Aaron ___ |
| V - 4. CAULKING | D. He escaped slavery and became a great orator. |
| S - 5. HIRING | E. Douglass's last name at birth |
| B - 6. AULD | F. Douglass attributed his good fortune to ___. |
| Y - 7. GORE | G. Was cursed in the Bible; slaves supposedly descended from him |
| G - 8. HAM | H. Douglass worked here when he learned to write. |
| J - 9. ANNA | I. Month of Douglass's final escape |
| O - 10. MULATTO | J. Douglass's wife |
| D - 11. FREDERICK | K. The Colonel used it to keep slaves out of the garden. |
| H - 12. SHIPYARD | L. Served by the slaveholding religion |
| U - 13. ROOT | M. Done when slaves were unhappy, not happy as believed |
| T - 14. ESCAPE | N. Slave who gave Douglass the root |
| I - 15. SEPTEMBER | O. Child with slave mother and white father |
| A - 16. TUCKAHOE | P. Douglass's age when his mother died |
| N - 17. JENKINS | Q. David who helped Douglass in New York |
| F - 18. GOD | R. Location of anti-slavery meeting where Douglass first spoke |
| X - 19. HICK | S. Douglass considered it as a step towards freedom: ___ out |
| C - 20. ANTHONY | T. This was easier to do from the city. |
| Q - 21. RUGGLES | U. Supposed to keep slaves from being whipped: lucky ___ |
| K - 22. TAR | V. Douglass's learned trade, done to ships |
| R - 23. NANTUCKET | W. Douglass copied letters on it to learn to write. |
| P - 24. SEVEN | X. Murdered Douglass's wife's cousin |
| L - 25. DEVIL | Y. Cruel; gave severe punishments |

Frederick Douglass Matching 3

___ 1. SHIPYARD
___ 2. BALTIMORE
___ 3. RELIGIOUS
___ 4. SEPTEMBER
___ 5. TUCKAHOE
___ 6. CAULKING
___ 7. COLUMBIAN
___ 8. LIBERATOR
___ 9. GORE
___ 10. SEVEN
___ 11. BEAL
___ 12. ESCAPE
___ 13. GRANDMOTHER
___ 14. MULATTO
___ 15. HAM
___ 16. TIMBER
___ 17. ANTHONY
___ 18. ABOLITIONISTS
___ 19. SINGING
___ 20. DEMBY
___ 21. BREAD
___ 22. JOHNSON
___ 23. TAR
___ 24. COVEY
___ 25. AULD

A. Douglass's learned trade, done to ships
B. Douglass traded it for reading lessons from white boys.
C. Douglass's age when his mother died
D. Paper Douglass began reading in New York
E. Douglass's white father, clerk to Lloyd: Aaron ___
F. Done when slaves were unhappy, not happy as believed
G. Douglass lived there with Hugh Auld.
H. Slave breaker Douglass eventually beat
I. Slaveholders of the worst kind had this quality.
J. Douglass's birthplace
K. Reading The ___ Orator helped Douglass argue against slavery.
L. Taught Douglass some of the alphabet and spelling
M. Last name Douglass used in New York
N. The Colonel used it to keep slaves out of the garden.
O. She raised Frederick after he was taken from his mother.
P. Douglass learned about these anti-slavery people from the newspaper
Q. This was easier to do from the city.
R. Month of Douglass's final escape
S. Was cursed in the Bible; slaves supposedly descended from him
T. Douglass copied letters on it to learn to write.
U. Shot and killed a slave with a musket: ___ Bondy
V. Douglass worked here when he learned to write.
W. Shot by Gore
X. Cruel; gave severe punishments
Y. Child with slave mother and white father

Frederick Douglass Matching 3 Answer Key

V - 1. SHIPYARD
G - 2. BALTIMORE
I - 3. RELIGIOUS
R - 4. SEPTEMBER
J - 5. TUCKAHOE
A - 6. CAULKING
K - 7. COLUMBIAN
D - 8. LIBERATOR
X - 9. GORE
C - 10. SEVEN
U - 11. BEAL
Q - 12. ESCAPE
O - 13. GRANDMOTHER
Y - 14. MULATTO
S - 15. HAM
T - 16. TIMBER
E - 17. ANTHONY
P - 18. ABOLITIONISTS
F - 19. SINGING
W - 20. DEMBY
B - 21. BREAD
M - 22. JOHNSON
N - 23. TAR
H - 24. COVEY
L - 25. AULD

A. Douglass's learned trade, done to ships
B. Douglass traded it for reading lessons from white boys.
C. Douglass's age when his mother died
D. Paper Douglass began reading in New York
E. Douglass's white father, clerk to Lloyd: Aaron ___
F. Done when slaves were unhappy, not happy as believed
G. Douglass lived there with Hugh Auld.
H. Slave breaker Douglass eventually beat
I. Slaveholders of the worst kind had this quality.
J. Douglass's birthplace
K. Reading The ___ Orator helped Douglass argue against slavery.
L. Taught Douglass some of the alphabet and spelling
M. Last name Douglass used in New York
N. The Colonel used it to keep slaves out of the garden.
O. She raised Frederick after he was taken from his mother.
P. Douglass learned about these anti-slavery people from the newspaper
Q. This was easier to do from the city.
R. Month of Douglass's final escape
S. Was cursed in the Bible; slaves supposedly descended from him
T. Douglass copied letters on it to learn to write.
U. Shot and killed a slave with a musket: ___ Bondy
V. Douglass worked here when he learned to write.
W. Shot by Gore
X. Cruel; gave severe punishments
Y. Child with slave mother and white father

Frederick Douglass Matching 4

___ 1. NANTUCKET
___ 2. SIX
___ 3. SEVEN
___ 4. THOMAS
___ 5. BALTIMORE
___ 6. ESCAPE
___ 7. SINGING
___ 8. SEPTEMBER
___ 9. BIRTH
___ 10. COLUMBIAN
___ 11. SHIPYARD
___ 12. DOUGLASS
___ 13. HIRING
___ 14. ANNA
___ 15. HARRIET
___ 16. GOD
___ 17. JENKINS
___ 18. DANIEL
___ 19. COVEY
___ 20. HAM
___ 21. BREAD
___ 22. FREDERICK
___ 23. RUGGLES
___ 24. BAILEY
___ 25. BEDFORD

A. Douglass moved here from New York: New ___
B. Lloyd who protected Frederick from older boys
C. David who helped Douglass in New York
D. Reading The ___ Orator helped Douglass argue against slavery.
E. 1818 is the estimated year of Douglass's ___.
F. Number of cents Hugh Auld gave Douglass from his wages
G. Did not give slaves enough to eat: Master ___
H. Slave breaker Douglass eventually beat
I. Douglass worked here when he learned to write.
J. He escaped slavery and became a great orator.
K. Was cursed in the Bible; slaves supposedly descended from him
L. Douglass's age when his mother died
M. This was easier to do from the city.
N. Douglass considered it as a step towards freedom: ___ out
O. Douglass lived there with Hugh Auld.
P. Done when slaves were unhappy, not happy as believed
Q. Douglass traded it for reading lessons from white boys.
R. Month of Douglass's final escape
S. Douglass's mother
T. Douglass's last name at birth
U. Slave who gave Douglass the root
V. Douglass attributed his good fortune to ___.
W. Douglass's wife
X. Location of anti-slavery meeting where Douglass first spoke
Y. Name came from the book Lady of the Lake

Frederick Douglass Matching 4 Answer Key

X - 1. NANTUCKET
F - 2. SIX
L - 3. SEVEN
G - 4. THOMAS
O - 5. BALTIMORE
M - 6. ESCAPE
P - 7. SINGING
R - 8. SEPTEMBER
E - 9. BIRTH
D - 10. COLUMBIAN
I - 11. SHIPYARD
Y - 12. DOUGLASS
N - 13. HIRING
W - 14. ANNA
S - 15. HARRIET
V - 16. GOD
U - 17. JENKINS
B - 18. DANIEL
H - 19. COVEY
K - 20. HAM
Q - 21. BREAD
J - 22. FREDERICK
C - 23. RUGGLES
T - 24. BAILEY
A - 25. BEDFORD

A. Douglass moved here from New York: New ___
B. Lloyd who protected Frederick from older boys
C. David who helped Douglass in New York
D. Reading The ___ Orator helped Douglass argue against slavery.
E. 1818 is the estimated year of Douglass's ___.
F. Number of cents Hugh Auld gave Douglass from his wages
G. Did not give slaves enough to eat: Master ___
H. Slave breaker Douglass eventually beat
I. Douglass worked here when he learned to write.
J. He escaped slavery and became a great orator.
K. Was cursed in the Bible; slaves supposedly descended from him
L. Douglass's age when his mother died
M. This was easier to do from the city.
N. Douglass considered it as a step towards freedom: ___ out
O. Douglass lived there with Hugh Auld.
P. Done when slaves were unhappy, not happy as believed
Q. Douglass traded it for reading lessons from white boys.
R. Month of Douglass's final escape
S. Douglass's mother
T. Douglass's last name at birth
U. Slave who gave Douglass the root
V. Douglass attributed his good fortune to ___.
W. Douglass's wife
X. Location of anti-slavery meeting where Douglass first spoke
Y. Name came from the book Lady of the Lake

Frederick Douglass Magic Squares 1

Match the definition with the vocabulary word. Put your answers in the magic squares below. When your answers are correct, all columns and rows will add to the same number.

A. BEDFORD
B. ROOT
C. BREAD
D. ABOLITIONISTS
E. NANTUCKET
F. DANIEL
G. GOD
H. LIBERATOR
I. BALTIMORE
J. SEPTEMBER
K. FREDERICK
L. DEMBY
M. SIX
N. BAILEY
O. LANMAN
P. COLUMBIAN

1. Supposed to keep slaves from being whipped: lucky ___
2. Douglass attributed his good fortune to ___.
3. He escaped slavery and became a great orator.
4. Douglass's last name at birth
5. Number of cents Hugh Auld gave Douglass from his wages
6. Shot by Gore
7. Paper Douglass began reading in New York
8. Douglass moved here from New York: New ___
9. Reading The ___ Orator helped Douglass argue against slavery.
10. Douglass lived there with Hugh Auld.
11. Location of anti-slavery meeting where Douglass first spoke
12. Douglass learned about these anti-slavery people from the newspaper
13. Douglass traded it for reading lessons from white boys.
14. Lloyd who protected Frederick from older boys
15. Month of Douglass's final escape
16. Killed two slaves, one with a hatchet

| A= | B= | C= | D= |
| --- | --- | --- | --- |
| E= | F= | G= | H= |
| I= | J= | K= | L= |
| M= | N= | O= | P= |

Frederick Douglass Magic Squares 1 Answer Key

Match the definition with the vocabulary word. Put your answers in the magic squares below. When your answers are correct, all columns and rows will add to the same number.

A. BEDFORD
B. ROOT
C. BREAD
D. ABOLITIONISTS
E. NANTUCKET
F. DANIEL
G. GOD
H. LIBERATOR
I. BALTIMORE
J. SEPTEMBER
K. FREDERICK
L. DEMBY
M. SIX
N. BAILEY
O. LANMAN
P. COLUMBIAN

1. Supposed to keep slaves from being whipped: lucky ___
2. Douglass attributed his good fortune to ___.
3. He escaped slavery and became a great orator.
4. Douglass's last name at birth
5. Number of cents Hugh Auld gave Douglass from his wages
6. Shot by Gore
7. Paper Douglass began reading in New York
8. Douglass moved here from New York: New ___
9. Reading The ___ Orator helped Douglass argue against slavery.
10. Douglass lived there with Hugh Auld.
11. Location of anti-slavery meeting where Douglass first spoke
12. Douglass learned about these anti-slavery people from the newspaper
13. Douglass traded it for reading lessons from white boys.
14. Lloyd who protected Frederick from older boys
15. Month of Douglass's final escape
16. Killed two slaves, one with a hatchet

| A=8 | B=1 | C=13 | D=12 |
| --- | --- | --- | --- |
| E=11 | F=14 | G=2 | H=7 |
| I=10 | J=15 | K=3 | L=6 |
| M=5 | N=4 | O=16 | P=9 |

Frederick Douglass Magic Squares 2

Match the definition with the vocabulary word. Put your answers in the magic squares below. When your answers are correct, all columns and rows will add to the same number.

A. BIRTH
B. ABOLITIONISTS
C. TIMBER
D. SEVEN
E. DEMBY
F. COVEY
G. ARTFUL
H. HICK
I. LIBERATOR
J. SEPTEMBER
K. BAILEY
L. BALTIMORE
M. CAULKING
N. BEAL
O. FREDERICK
P. SHIPYARD

1. He escaped slavery and became a great orator.
2. Douglass's age when his mother died
3. Month of Douglass's final escape
4. Shot by Gore
5. Paper Douglass began reading in New York
6. Slave breaker Douglass eventually beat
7. Douglass worked here when he learned to write.
8. Douglass copied letters on it to learn to write.
9. Murdered Douglass's wife's cousin
10. Douglass's last name at birth
11. 1818 is the estimated year of Douglass's ___.
12. Shot and killed a slave with a musket: ___ Bondy
13. Douglass learned about these anti-slavery people from the newspaper
14. Douglass's learned trade, done to ships
15. Douglass described Mr. Gore as cruel, ___, and obdurate.
16. Douglass lived there with Hugh Auld.

| A= | B= | C= | D= |
| E= | F= | G= | H= |
| I= | J= | K= | L= |
| M= | N= | O= | P= |

Frederick Douglass Magic Squares 2 Answer Key

Match the definition with the vocabulary word. Put your answers in the magic squares below. When your answers are correct, all columns and rows will add to the same number.

A. BIRTH
B. ABOLITIONISTS
C. TIMBER
D. SEVEN
E. DEMBY
F. COVEY
G. ARTFUL
H. HICK
I. LIBERATOR
J. SEPTEMBER
K. BAILEY
L. BALTIMORE
M. CAULKING
N. BEAL
O. FREDERICK
P. SHIPYARD

1. He escaped slavery and became a great orator.
2. Douglass's age when his mother died
3. Month of Douglass's final escape
4. Shot by Gore
5. Paper Douglass began reading in New York
6. Slave breaker Douglass eventually beat
7. Douglass worked here when he learned to write.
8. Douglass copied letters on it to learn to write.
9. Murdered Douglass's wife's cousin
10. Douglass's last name at birth
11. 1818 is the estimated year of Douglass's ___.
12. Shot and killed a slave with a musket: ___ Bondy
13. Douglass learned about these anti-slavery people from the newspaper
14. Douglass's learned trade, done to ships
15. Douglass described Mr. Gore as cruel, ___, and obdurate.
16. Douglass lived there with Hugh Auld.

| A=11 | B=13 | C=8 | D=2 |
|---|---|---|---|
| E=4 | F=6 | G=15 | H=9 |
| I=5 | J=3 | K=10 | L=16 |
| M=14 | N=12 | O=1 | P=7 |

Frederick Douglass Magic Squares 3

Match the definition with the vocabulary word. Put your answers in the magic squares below. When your answers are correct, all columns and rows will add to the same number.

A. TAR
B. TUCKAHOE
C. ARTFUL
D. BEAL
E. RUGGLES
F. CAULKING
G. BAILEY
H. ESCAPE
I. BIRTH
J. DANIEL
K. JOHNSON
L. ANNA
M. HAM
N. GRANDMOTHER
O. COVEY
P. HICK

1. This was easier to do from the city.
2. Was cursed in the Bible; slaves supposedly descended from him
3. Douglass's birthplace
4. Last name Douglass used in New York
5. Lloyd who protected Frederick from older boys
6. Douglass described Mr. Gore as cruel, ___, and obdurate.
7. Murdered Douglass's wife's cousin
8. David who helped Douglass in New York
9. Slave breaker Douglass eventually beat
10. Douglass's learned trade, done to ships
11. 1818 is the estimated year of Douglass's ___.
12. Shot and killed a slave with a musket: ___ Bondy
13. The Colonel used it to keep slaves out of the garden.
14. Douglass's wife
15. Douglass's last name at birth
16. She raised Frederick after he was taken from his mother.

| A= | B= | C= | D= |
|---|---|---|---|
| E= | F= | G= | H= |
| I= | J= | K= | L= |
| M= | N= | O= | P= |

25
Copyrighted

Frederick Douglass Magic Squares 3 Answer Key

Match the definition with the vocabulary word. Put your answers in the magic squares below. When your answers are correct, all columns and rows will add to the same number.

A. TAR
B. TUCKAHOE
C. ARTFUL
D. BEAL
E. RUGGLES
F. CAULKING
G. BAILEY
H. ESCAPE
I. BIRTH
J. DANIEL
K. JOHNSON
L. ANNA
M. HAM
N. GRANDMOTHER
O. COVEY
P. HICK

1. This was easier to do from the city.
2. Was cursed in the Bible; slaves supposedly descended from him
3. Douglass's birthplace
4. Last name Douglass used in New York
5. Lloyd who protected Frederick from older boys
6. Douglass described Mr. Gore as cruel, ___, and obdurate.
7. Murdered Douglass's wife's cousin
8. David who helped Douglass in New York
9. Slave breaker Douglass eventually beat
10. Douglass's learned trade, done to ships
11. 1818 is the estimated year of Douglass's ___.
12. Shot and killed a slave with a musket: ___ Bondy
13. The Colonel used it to keep slaves out of the garden.
14. Douglass's wife
15. Douglass's last name at birth
16. She raised Frederick after he was taken from his mother.

| A=13 | B=3 | C=6 | D=12 |
| --- | --- | --- | --- |
| E=8 | F=10 | G=15 | H=1 |
| I=11 | J=5 | K=4 | L=14 |
| M=2 | N=16 | O=9 | P=7 |

Frederick Douglass Magic Squares 4

Match the definition with the vocabulary word. Put your answers in the magic squares below. When your answers are correct, all columns and rows will add to the same number.

A. MULATTO
B. COVEY
C. RUGGLES
D. RELIGIOUS
E. LIBERATOR
F. BEDFORD
G. GORE
H. BEAL
I. SEVEN
J. BREAD
K. BALTIMORE
L. DOUGLASS
M. NANTUCKET
N. FREDERICK
O. GOD
P. DANIEL

1. Douglass moved here from New York: New ___
2. Douglass's age when his mother died
3. Douglass attributed his good fortune to ___.
4. Slaveholders of the worst kind had this quality.
5. Location of anti-slavery meeting where Douglass first spoke
6. Slave breaker Douglass eventually beat
7. Shot and killed a slave with a musket: ___ Bondy
8. Douglass lived there with Hugh Auld.
9. David who helped Douglass in New York
10. Lloyd who protected Frederick from older boys
11. Douglass traded it for reading lessons from white boys.
12. Paper Douglass began reading in New York
13. Name came from the book Lady of the Lake
14. Cruel; gave severe punishments
15. Child with slave mother and white father
16. He escaped slavery and became a great orator.

| A= | B= | C= | D= |
| E= | F= | G= | H= |
| I= | J= | K= | L= |
| M= | N= | O= | P= |

Frederick Douglass Magic Squares 4 Answer Key

Match the definition with the vocabulary word. Put your answers in the magic squares below. When your answers are correct, all columns and rows will add to the same number.

A. MULATTO
B. COVEY
C. RUGGLES
D. RELIGIOUS
E. LIBERATOR
F. BEDFORD
G. GORE
H. BEAL
I. SEVEN
J. BREAD
K. BALTIMORE
L. DOUGLASS
M. NANTUCKET
N. FREDERICK
O. GOD
P. DANIEL

1. Douglass moved here from New York: New ___
2. Douglass's age when his mother died
3. Douglass attributed his good fortune to ___.
4. Slaveholders of the worst kind had this quality.
5. Location of anti-slavery meeting where Douglass first spoke
6. Slave breaker Douglass eventually beat
7. Shot and killed a slave with a musket: ___ Bondy
8. Douglass lived there with Hugh Auld.
9. David who helped Douglass in New York
10. Lloyd who protected Frederick from older boys
11. Douglass traded it for reading lessons from white boys.
12. Paper Douglass began reading in New York
13. Name came from the book Lady of the Lake
14. Cruel; gave severe punishments
15. Child with slave mother and white father
16. He escaped slavery and became a great orator.

| A=15 | B=6 | C=9 | D=4 |
| --- | --- | --- | --- |
| E=12 | F=1 | G=14 | H=7 |
| I=2 | J=11 | K=8 | L=13 |
| M=5 | N=16 | O=3 | P=10 |

# Frederick Douglass Word Search 1

```
J N T G B T A N T H O N Y E V O C C
O A U G B E Q F A L I B E R A T O R
H N C F J R A R J R M R N S Q Y L D
N T K C I H R L D E F L I I C C U P
S U A V D I F R D B N D B N M W M L
O C H B E F X Z J Z A K T G G P B H
N K O T E R M P C E D M I I M T I V
R E E R C D G O R E A U R N M P A C
E T L S S A F B L L N L U G S B N R
L F L P E M U O V G I A G B V I E N
I Y O J T V H L R O E T G X Z R G R
G F Y M E Y E J K D L T L U F T R A
I Y D D E S X N L I V O E A B H O Y
O S N L S G C I G Z N M S D N W O X
U B I V W R V A N N A G L B M M T V
S A B X R E G K P H M U T J T J A M
B T J Z D Z W X J E A T H O M A S N
```

1818 is the estimated year of Douglass's ___. (5)
Child with slave mother and white father (7)
Col. who owned the plantation where Douglass first lived (5)
Cruel; gave severe punishments (4)
David who helped Douglass in New York (7)
Did not give slaves enough to eat: Master ___ (6)
Done when slaves were unhappy, not happy as believed (7)
Douglass attributed his good fortune to ___. (3)
Douglass considered it as a step towards freedom: ___ out (6)
Douglass copied letters on it to learn to write. (6)
Douglass described Mr. Gore as cruel, ___, and obdurate. (6)
Douglass moved here from New York: New ___ (7)
Douglass traded it for reading lessons from white boys. (5)
Douglass's age when his mother died (5)
Douglass's birthplace (8)
Douglass's last name at birth (6)
Douglass's learned trade, done to ships (8)
Douglass's mother (7)
Douglass's white father, clerk to Lloyd: Aaron ___ (7)
Douglass's wife (4)
Killed two slaves, one with a hatchet (6)
Last name Douglass used in New York (7)
Lloyd who protected Frederick from older boys (6)
Location of anti-slavery meeting where Douglass first spoke (9)
Murdered Douglass's wife's cousin (4)
Number of cents Hugh Auld gave Douglass from his wages (3)
Paper Douglass began reading in New York (9)
Reading The ___ Orator helped Douglass argue against slavery. (9)
Served by the slaveholding religion (5)
Shot and killed a slave with a musket: ___ Bondy (4)
Shot by Gore (5)
Slave breaker Douglass eventually beat (5)
Slave who gave Douglass the root (7)
Slaveholders of the worst kind had this quality. (9)
Supposed to keep slaves from being whipped: lucky ___ (4)
Taught Douglass some of the alphabet and spelling (4)
The Colonel used it to keep slaves out of the garden. (3)
This was easier to do from the city. (6)
Was cursed in the Bible; slaves supposedly descended from him (3)

# Frederick Douglass Word Search 1 Answer Key

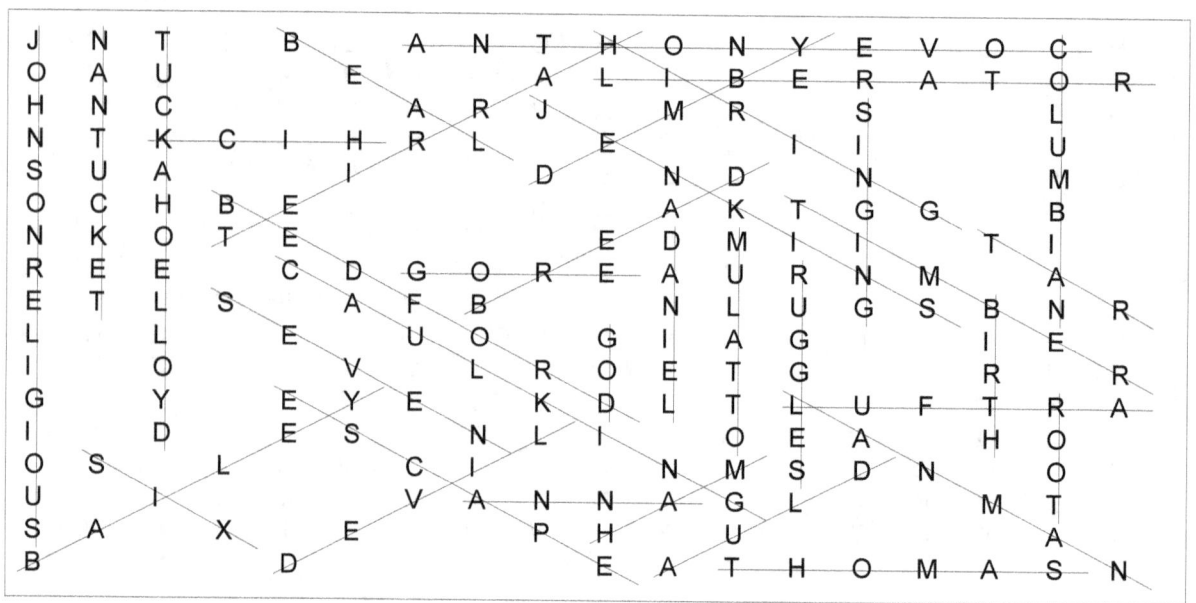

1818 is the estimated year of Douglass's ___. (5)
Child with slave mother and white father (7)
Col. who owned the plantation where Douglass first lived (5)
Cruel; gave severe punishments (4)
David who helped Douglass in New York (7)
Did not give slaves enough to eat: Master ___ (6)
Done when slaves were unhappy, not happy as believed (7)
Douglass attributed his good fortune to ___. (3)
Douglass considered it as a step towards freedom: ___ out (6)
Douglass copied letters on it to learn to write. (6)
Douglass described Mr. Gore as cruel, ___, and obdurate. (6)
Douglass moved here from New York: New ___ (7)
Douglass traded it for reading lessons from white boys. (5)
Douglass's age when his mother died (5)
Douglass's birthplace (8)
Douglass's last name at birth (6)
Douglass's learned trade, done to ships (8)
Douglass's mother (7)
Douglass's white father, clerk to Lloyd: Aaron ___ (7)
Douglass's wife (4)

Killed two slaves, one with a hatchet (6)
Last name Douglass used in New York (7)
Lloyd who protected Frederick from older boys (6)
Location of anti-slavery meeting where Douglass first spoke (9)
Murdered Douglass's wife's cousin (4)
Number of cents Hugh Auld gave Douglass from his wages (3)
Paper Douglass began reading in New York (9)
Reading The ___ Orator helped Douglass argue against slavery. (9)
Served by the slaveholding religion (5)
Shot and killed a slave with a musket: ___ Bondy (4)
Shot by Gore (5)
Slave breaker Douglass eventually beat (5)
Slave who gave Douglass the root (7)
Slaveholders of the worst kind had this quality. (9)
Supposed to keep slaves from being whipped: lucky ___ (4)
Taught Douglass some of the alphabet and spelling (4)
The Colonel used it to keep slaves out of the garden. (3)
This was easier to do from the city. (6)
Was cursed in the Bible; slaves supposedly descended from him (3)

30
Copyrighted

# Frederick Douglass Word Search 2

```
H A R R I E T D S S A L G U O D Y L
J I K R G S H I P Y A R D N A R B Q
G C C A N T H O N Y L B T N F O A Q
H C P K I U R K B A Y S I F J O L Y
S L Z M G C U K E L N E W B U T T D
S X P U N K G B V D L G Q Y T L I Z
A Q M L I A G S L Q E V S B A L M X
M H M A S H L B E P B V Q A U O O Y
O A N T H O E H K V R T I I L Y R R
H R A D E S C A P E N G L D D E W
T R R O I N L D H K A N O E Y B L G
L I G L I M R A C I D G R Y M W I Z
B Q L K Y O B U N S R A E E S C G P
D P N B F K T E K M N I T L I O I S
Q E M D V N L M R N A P N J X V O C
J E E G A K S G A Q E N Z G Y E U X
D B T N B N V N O S N H O J F Y S H
```

1818 is the estimated year of Douglass's ___. (5)
Child with slave mother and white father (7)
Col. who owned the plantation where Douglass first lived (5)
Cruel; gave severe punishments (4)
David who helped Douglass in New York (7)
Did not give slaves enough to eat: Master ___ (6)
Done when slaves were unhappy, not happy as believed (7)
Douglass attributed his good fortune to ___. (3)
Douglass considered it as a step towards freedom: ___ out (6)
Douglass copied letters on it to learn to write. (6)
Douglass described Mr. Gore as cruel, ___, and obdurate. (6)
Douglass lived there with Hugh Auld. (9)
Douglass moved here from New York: New ___ (7)
Douglass traded it for reading lessons from white boys. (5)
Douglass worked here when he learned to write. (8)
Douglass's age when his mother died (5)
Douglass's birthplace (8)
Douglass's last name at birth (6)
Douglass's mother (7)
Douglass's white father, clerk to Lloyd: Aaron ___ (7)
Douglass's wife (4)
Killed two slaves, one with a hatchet (6)
Last name Douglass used in New York (7)
Lloyd who protected Frederick from older boys (6)
Location of anti-slavery meeting where Douglass first spoke (9)
Month of Douglass's final escape (9)
Murdered Douglass's wife's cousin (4)
Name came from the book Lady of the Lake (8)
Number of cents Hugh Auld gave Douglass from his wages (3)
Served by the slaveholding religion (5)
Shot and killed a slave with a musket: ___ Bondy (4)
Shot by Gore (5)
Slave breaker Douglass eventually beat (5)
Slave who gave Douglass the root (7)
Slaveholders of the worst kind had this quality. (9)
Supposed to keep slaves from being whipped: lucky ___ (4)
Taught Douglass some of the alphabet and spelling (4)
The Colonel used it to keep slaves out of the garden. (3)
This was easier to do from the city. (6)
Was cursed in the Bible; slaves supposedly descended from him (3)

Frederick Douglass Word Search 2 Answer Key

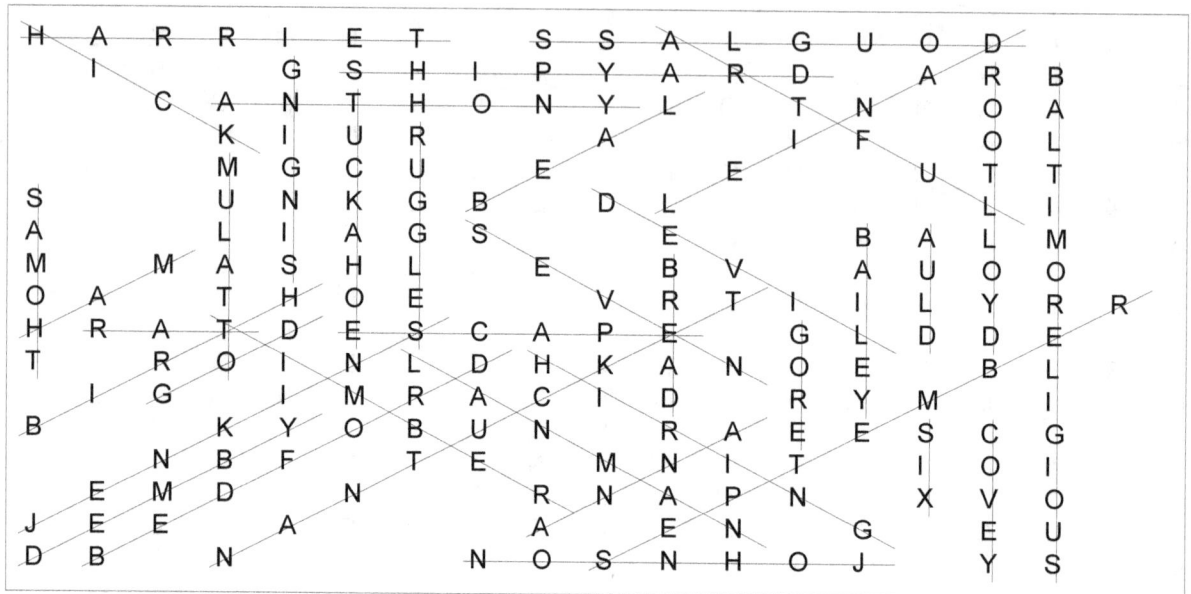

1818 is the estimated year of Douglass's ___. (5)
Child with slave mother and white father (7)
Col. who owned the plantation where Douglass first lived (5)
Cruel; gave severe punishments (4)
David who helped Douglass in New York (7)
Did not give slaves enough to eat: Master ___ (6)
Done when slaves were unhappy, not happy as believed (7)
Douglass attributed his good fortune to ___. (3)
Douglass considered it as a step towards freedom: ___ out (6)
Douglass copied letters on it to learn to write. (6)
Douglass described Mr. Gore as cruel, ___, and obdurate. (6)
Douglass lived there with Hugh Auld. (9)
Douglass moved here from New York: New ___ (7)
Douglass traded it for reading lessons from white boys. (5)
Douglass worked here when he learned to write. (8)
Douglass's age when his mother died (5)
Douglass's birthplace (8)
Douglass's last name at birth (6)
Douglass's mother (7)
Douglass's white father, clerk to Lloyd: Aaron ___ (7)
Douglass's wife (4)
Killed two slaves, one with a hatchet (6)
Last name Douglass used in New York (7)
Lloyd who protected Frederick from older boys (6)
Location of anti-slavery meeting where Douglass first spoke (9)
Month of Douglass's final escape (9)
Murdered Douglass's wife's cousin (4)
Name came from the book Lady of the Lake (8)
Number of cents Hugh Auld gave Douglass from his wages (3)
Served by the slaveholding religion (5)
Shot and killed a slave with a musket: ___ Bondy (4)
Shot by Gore (5)
Slave breaker Douglass eventually beat (5)
Slave who gave Douglass the root (7)
Slaveholders of the worst kind had this quality. (9)
Supposed to keep slaves from being whipped: lucky ___ (4)
Taught Douglass some of the alphabet and spelling (4)
The Colonel used it to keep slaves out of the garden. (3)
This was easier to do from the city. (6)
Was cursed in the Bible; slaves supposedly descended from him (3)

# Frederick Douglass Word Search 3

```
H P T H R C A U L K I N G N I G N I S H
W X P M V U J V H L I B E R A T O R R C L
F M Z T Z S G P B R B G K R F T Y L P C F
M S W C M L S G R K S H G F U R X D B H
C U Y H M J S Z L T K L D R C H X W J V
D J L F Y M A N B E R X M R K L Q B E X
A Q T A R X L K H E S C F C A Y G N N G
E F L X T H G X H B N H O J H J E H K Y
R J V J S T U T B S T A T V O V I F I Y
B A L T I M O R E D E M B Y E R O G N H
D K G S X M D P A R K P X S I Y O A S C
H Q Z W D L A Y L O C B T N W D I V Y B
Z T T N H C V F X F U Z G E N B X M S J
F D A T S A U L D D T T H O M A S T B M
W R R E Q N R W A E N W R U X B S L I B
G K Z Y F N V R N B A S L Y K I E G R K
L Z V V Q A B F I C N O P S N Y A R T Z
S H I P Y A R D E E C H U O D Z N O H L
W Y X K I R F E L D T O I Y N A T O Y K
X B F L B T N V D R I T O C M L H T Q B
Y W E C X F N I W G I L G N K Y O P N J
B Y H R Z U H L I L L J A J O H N S O N
B N X J B L B L O C F L R C S F Y B J N
N N J Z W B E B J V B D R J C C M Y R V
T I M B E R A S F R E D E R I C K N M T
```

| | | |
|---|---|---|
| ABOLITIONISTS | DEVIL | MULATTO |
| ANNA | DOUGLASS | NANTUCKET |
| ANTHONY | ESCAPE | RELIGIOUS |
| ARTFUL | FREDERICK | ROOT |
| AULD | GOD | RUGGLES |
| BAILEY | GORE | SEPTEMBER |
| BALTIMORE | GRANDMOTHER | SEVEN |
| BEAL | HAM | SHIPYARD |
| BEDFORD | HARRIET | SINGING |
| BIRTH | HICK | SIX |
| BREAD | HIRING | TAR |
| CAULKING | JENKINS | THOMAS |
| COLUMBIAN | JOHNSON | TIMBER |
| COVEY | LANMAN | TUCKAHOE |
| DANIEL | LIBERATOR | |
| DEMBY | LLOYD | |

Frederick Douglass Word Search 3 Answer Key

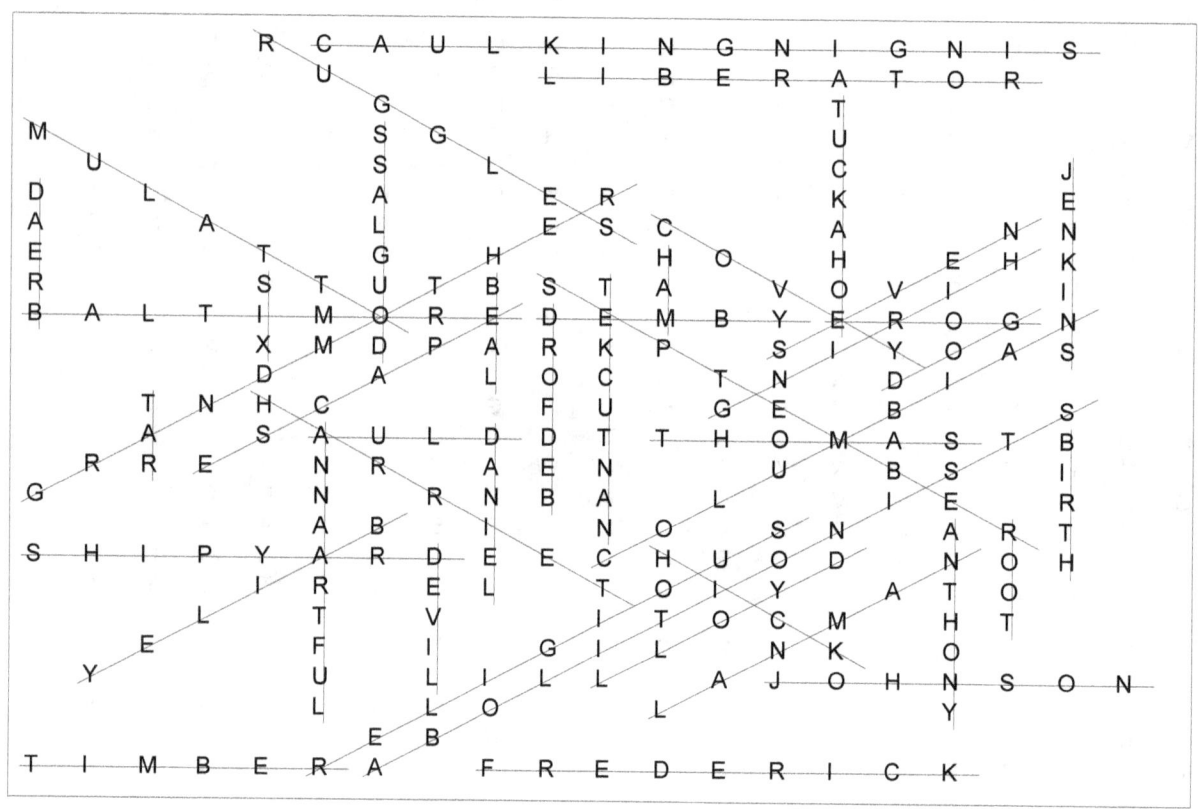

| ABOLITIONISTS | DEVIL | MULATTO |
| ANNA | DOUGLASS | NANTUCKET |
| ANTHONY | ESCAPE | RELIGIOUS |
| ARTFUL | FREDERICK | ROOT |
| AULD | GOD | RUGGLES |
| BAILEY | GORE | SEPTEMBER |
| BALTIMORE | GRANDMOTHER | SEVEN |
| BEAL | HAM | SHIPYARD |
| BEDFORD | HARRIET | SINGING |
| BIRTH | HICK | SIX |
| BREAD | HIRING | TAR |
| CAULKING | JENKINS | THOMAS |
| COLUMBIAN | JOHNSON | TIMBER |
| COVEY | LANMAN | TUCKAHOE |
| DANIEL | LIBERATOR | |
| DEMBY | LLOYD | |

# Frederick Douglass Word Search 4

```
S G T Y H L K S U O I G I L E R T A R L
H R B T I A K A E B L G O R C U O M N
I A D V R T M M T V V G O D T G W J K
P N E T I D P O K T E G T W B G K O T Z
Y D V B N C J H H A N N A A U L D L G
A M B J G B P T T J P I B M K E Y U L G
R O J E L M R J G E N K O V N S F G O N
D T M G A I L J P N F L L D G T S L Y D
K H V G B L F R R K R U I A R D I A D Y
T E J F P E V C Z I E A T A N P X S V N
L R W H T I K S R N D C I N V T T S D J
L A N M A N F W Y S E X O A N M H A Z H
H H L H R A Z E R I R H N N A M E O M S
A I I N F D V C H N I R I T I R S D N M
R C B S V O K Y T G C J S U B T E E O Y
R K E S C A P E B I K R T C M U P M S R
I T R F S Y F L A N M S S K U C T B N H
E Y A J P W D I L G X B R E L K E Y H Y
T B T K J R G A T Z K R E T O A M Q O Z
T V O S F Y V B I F M Y X R C H B J J J
C P R C F B W R M Z W T W Z G O E Q H W
Y F V H S R Y G O C M H K C B E R N M Y
M U L A T T O Z R S W G B E D F O R D T
Q W C G K S C Z E F B Q H L H B V W B R
F B K V G C R R N V B Z G H W Q Y B F V
```

ABOLITIONISTS
ANNA
ANTHONY
ARTFUL
AULD
BAILEY
BALTIMORE
BEAL
BEDFORD
BIRTH
BREAD
CAULKING
COLUMBIAN
COVEY
DANIEL
DEMBY

DEVIL
DOUGLASS
ESCAPE
FREDERICK
GOD
GORE
GRANDMOTHER
HAM
HARRIET
HICK
HIRING
JENKINS
JOHNSON
LANMAN
LIBERATOR
LLOYD

MULATTO
NANTUCKET
RELIGIOUS
ROOT
RUGGLES
SEPTEMBER
SEVEN
SHIPYARD
SINGING
SIX
TAR
THOMAS
TIMBER
TUCKAHOE

Frederick Douglass Word Search 4 Answer Key

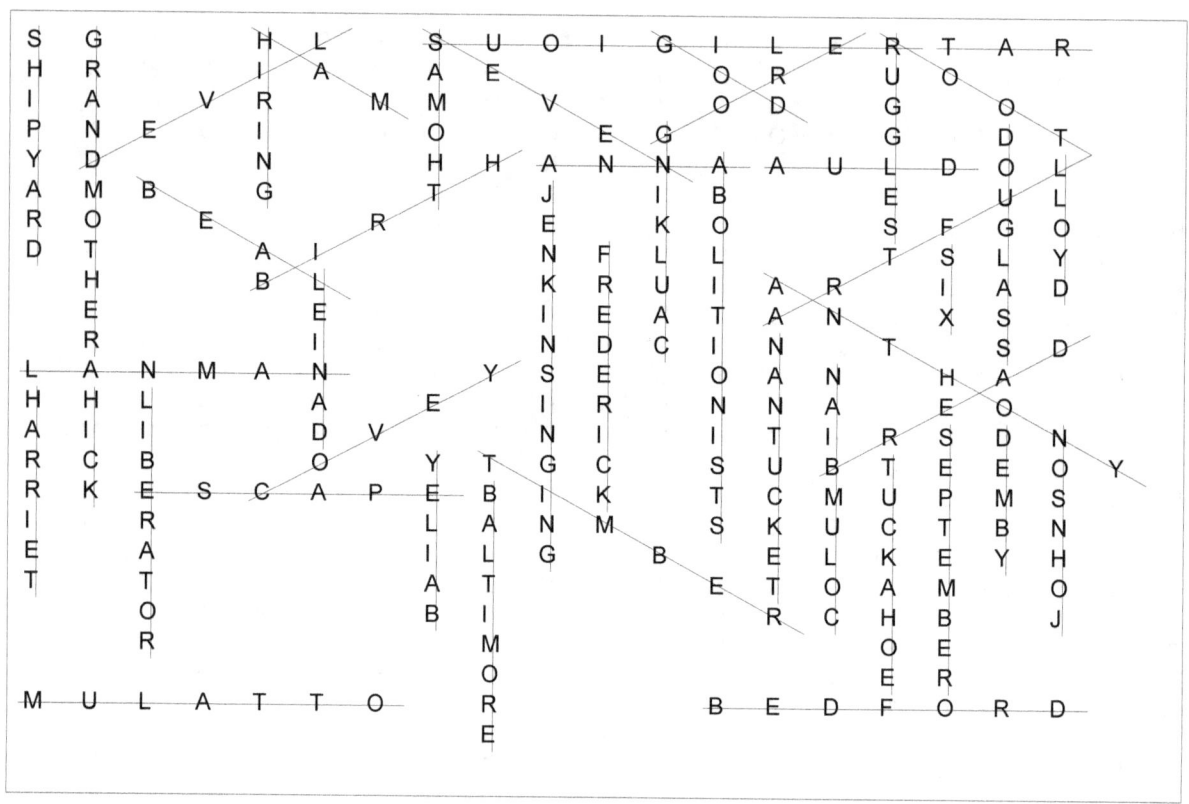

| ABOLITIONISTS | DEVIL | MULATTO |
| ANNA | DOUGLASS | NANTUCKET |
| ANTHONY | ESCAPE | RELIGIOUS |
| ARTFUL | FREDERICK | ROOT |
| AULD | GOD | RUGGLES |
| BAILEY | GORE | SEPTEMBER |
| BALTIMORE | GRANDMOTHER | SEVEN |
| BEAL | HAM | SHIPYARD |
| BEDFORD | HARRIET | SINGING |
| BIRTH | HICK | SIX |
| BREAD | HIRING | TAR |
| CAULKING | JENKINS | THOMAS |
| COLUMBIAN | JOHNSON | TIMBER |
| COVEY | LANMAN | TUCKAHOE |
| DANIEL | LIBERATOR | |
| DEMBY | LLOYD | |

# Frederick Douglass Crossword 1

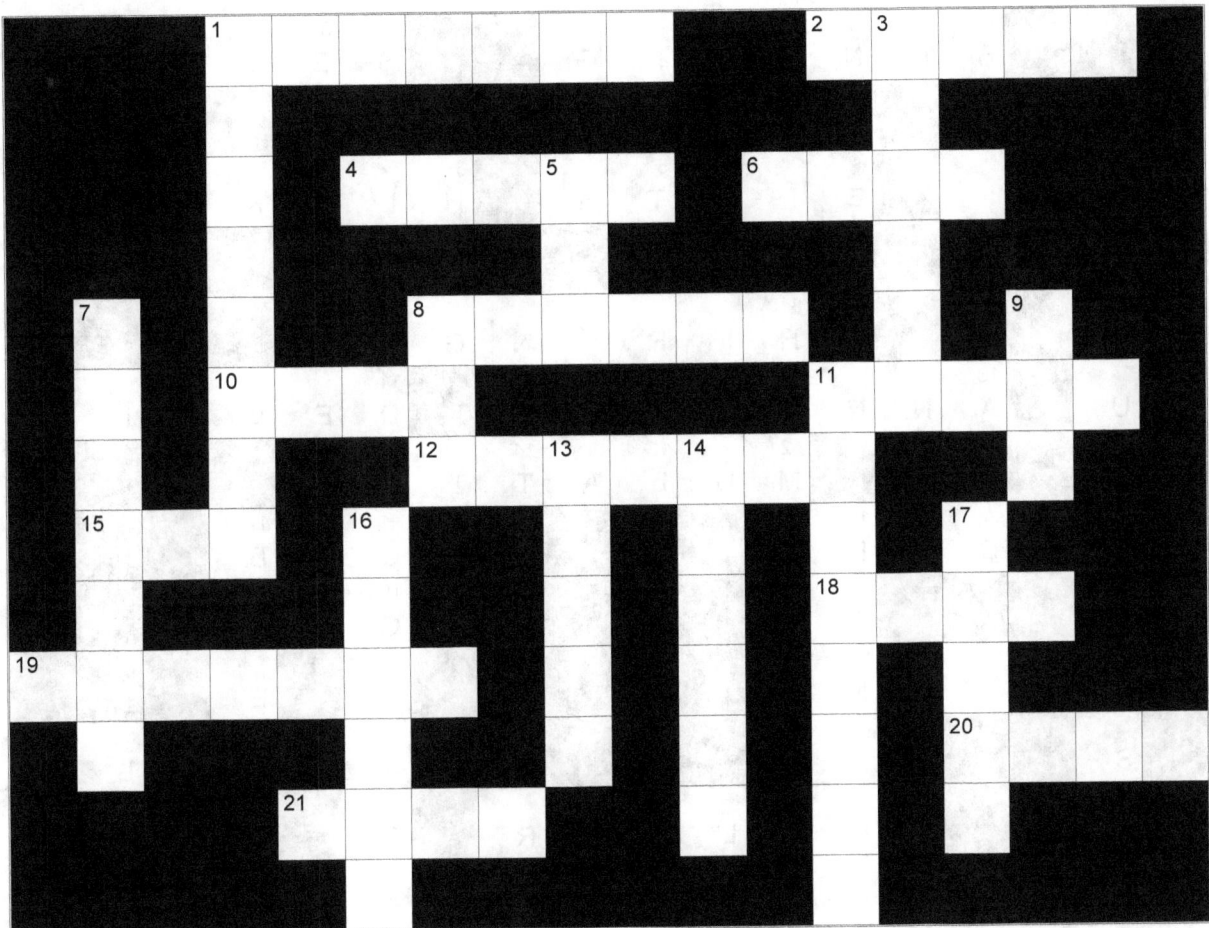

Across
1. Done when slaves were unhappy, not happy as believed
2. Douglass's age when his mother died
4. 1818 is the estimated year of Douglass's ___.
6. Murdered Douglass's wife's cousin
8. Douglass considered it as a step towards freedom: ___ out
10. Douglass's wife
11. Served by the slaveholding religion
12. Child with slave mother and white father
15. Douglass attributed his good fortune to ___.
18. Cruel; gave severe punishments
19. Slave who gave Douglass the root
20. Taught Douglass some of the alphabet and spelling
21. Shot and killed a slave with a musket: ___ Bondy

Down
1. Douglass worked here when he learned to write.
3. This was easier to do from the city.
5. The Colonel used it to keep slaves out of the garden.
7. David who helped Douglass in New York
8. Was cursed in the Bible; slaves supposedly descended from him
9. Number of cents Hugh Auld gave Douglass from his wages
11. Name came from the book Lady of the Lake
13. Col. who owned the plantation where Douglass first lived
14. Douglass copied letters on it to learn to write.
16. Lloyd who protected Frederick from older boys
17. Douglass traded it for reading lessons from white boys.

# Frederick Douglass Crossword 1 Answer Key

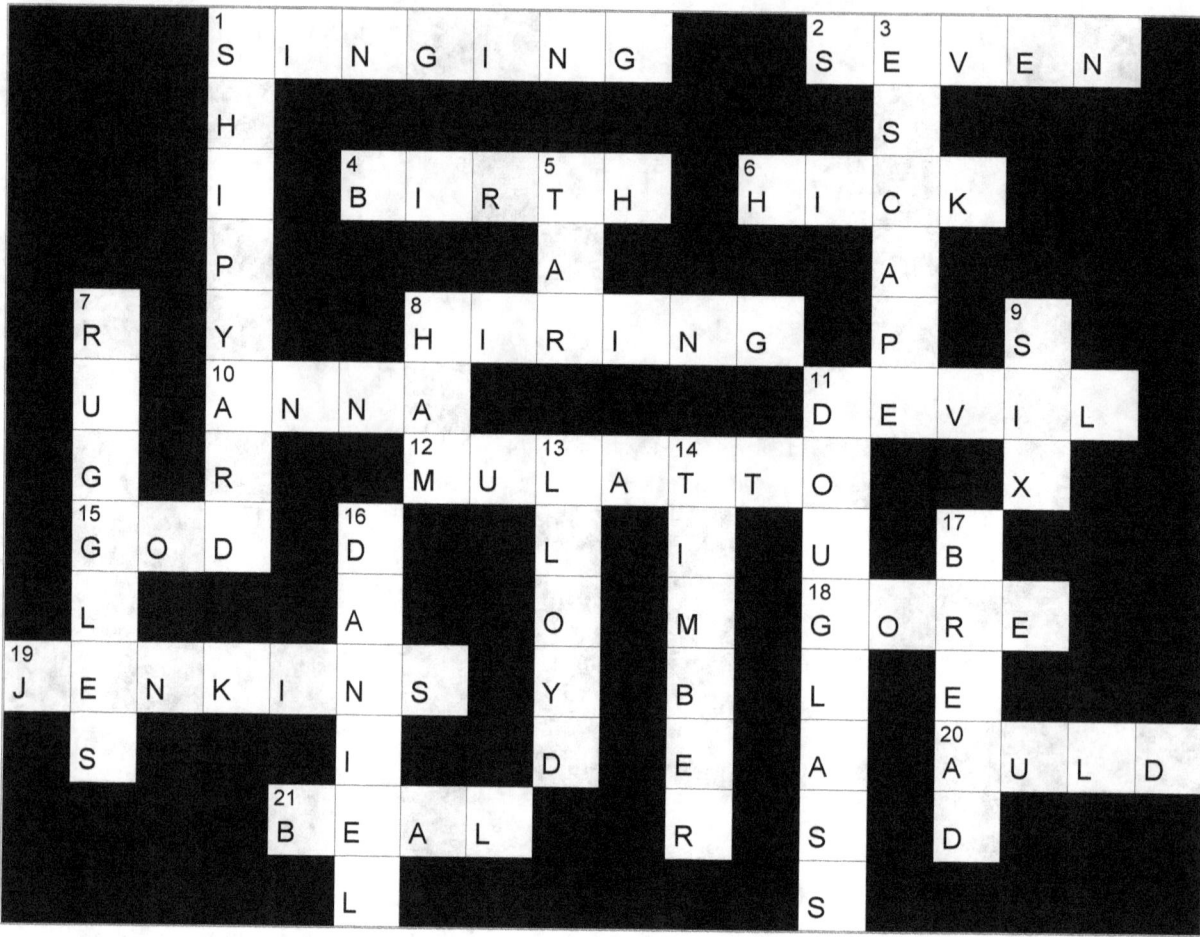

**Across**
1. Done when slaves were unhappy, not happy as believed
2. Douglass's age when his mother died
4. 1818 is the estimated year of Douglass's ___.
6. Murdered Douglass's wife's cousin
8. Douglass considered it as a step towards freedom: ___ out
10. Douglass's wife
11. Served by the slaveholding religion
12. Child with slave mother and white father
15. Douglass attributed his good fortune to ___.
18. Cruel; gave severe punishments
19. Slave who gave Douglass the root
20. Taught Douglass some of the alphabet and spelling
21. Shot and killed a slave with a musket: ___ Bondy

**Down**
1. Douglass worked here when he learned to write.
3. This was easier to do from the city.
5. The Colonel used it to keep slaves out of the garden.
7. David who helped Douglass in New York
8. Was cursed in the Bible; slaves supposedly descended from him
9. Number of cents Hugh Auld gave Douglass from his wages
11. Name came from the book Lady of the Lake
13. Col. who owned the plantation where Douglass first lived
14. Douglass copied letters on it to learn to write.
16. Lloyd who protected Frederick from older boys
17. Douglass traded it for reading lessons from white boys.

# Frederick Douglass Crossword 2

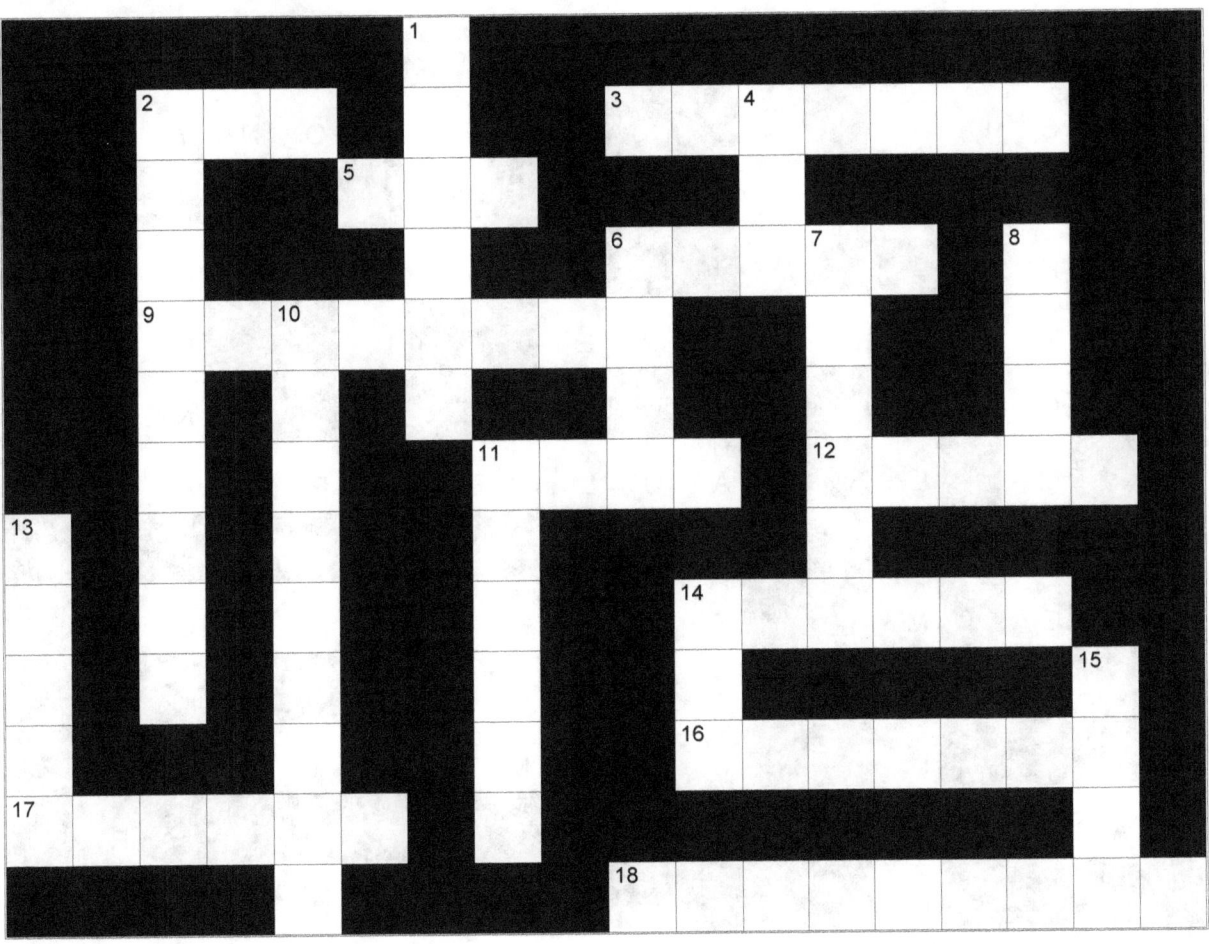

## Across
2. Number of cents Hugh Auld gave Douglass from his wages
3. Douglass's white father, clerk to Lloyd: Aaron ___
5. Douglass attributed his good fortune to ___.
6. 1818 is the estimated year of Douglass's ___.
9. Douglass's birthplace
11. Taught Douglass some of the alphabet and spelling
12. Douglass traded it for reading lessons from white boys.
14. Douglass considered it as a step towards freedom: ___ out
16. Child with slave mother and white father
17. Killed two slaves, one with a hatchet
18. Location of anti-slavery meeting where Douglass first spoke

## Down
1. Did not give slaves enough to eat: Master ___
2. Month of Douglass's final escape
4. The Colonel used it to keep slaves out of the garden.
6. Shot and killed a slave with a musket: ___ Bondy
7. Douglass copied letters on it to learn to write.
8. Douglass's wife
10. Reading The ___ Orator helped Douglass argue against slavery.
11. Douglass described Mr. Gore as cruel, ___, and obdurate.
13. Served by the slaveholding religion
14. Was cursed in the Bible; slaves supposedly descended from him
15. Cruel; gave severe punishments

# Frederick Douglass Crossword 2 Answer Key

**Across**
2. Number of cents Hugh Auld gave Douglass from his wages
3. Douglass's white father, clerk to Lloyd: Aaron ___
5. Douglass attributed his good fortune to ___.
6. 1818 is the estimated year of Douglass's ___.
9. Douglass's birthplace
11. Taught Douglass some of the alphabet and spelling
12. Douglass traded it for reading lessons from white boys.
14. Douglass considered it as a step towards freedom: ___ out
16. Child with slave mother and white father
17. Killed two slaves, one with a hatchet
18. Location of anti-slavery meeting where Douglass first spoke

**Down**
1. Did not give slaves enough to eat: Master ___
2. Month of Douglass's final escape
4. The Colonel used it to keep slaves out of the garden.
6. Shot and killed a slave with a musket: ___ Bondy
7. Douglass copied letters on it to learn to write.
8. Douglass's wife
10. Reading The ___ Orator helped Douglass argue against slavery.
11. Douglass described Mr. Gore as cruel, ___, and obdurate.
13. Served by the slaveholding religion
14. Was cursed in the Bible; slaves supposedly descended from him
15. Cruel; gave severe punishments

# Frederick Douglass Crossword 3

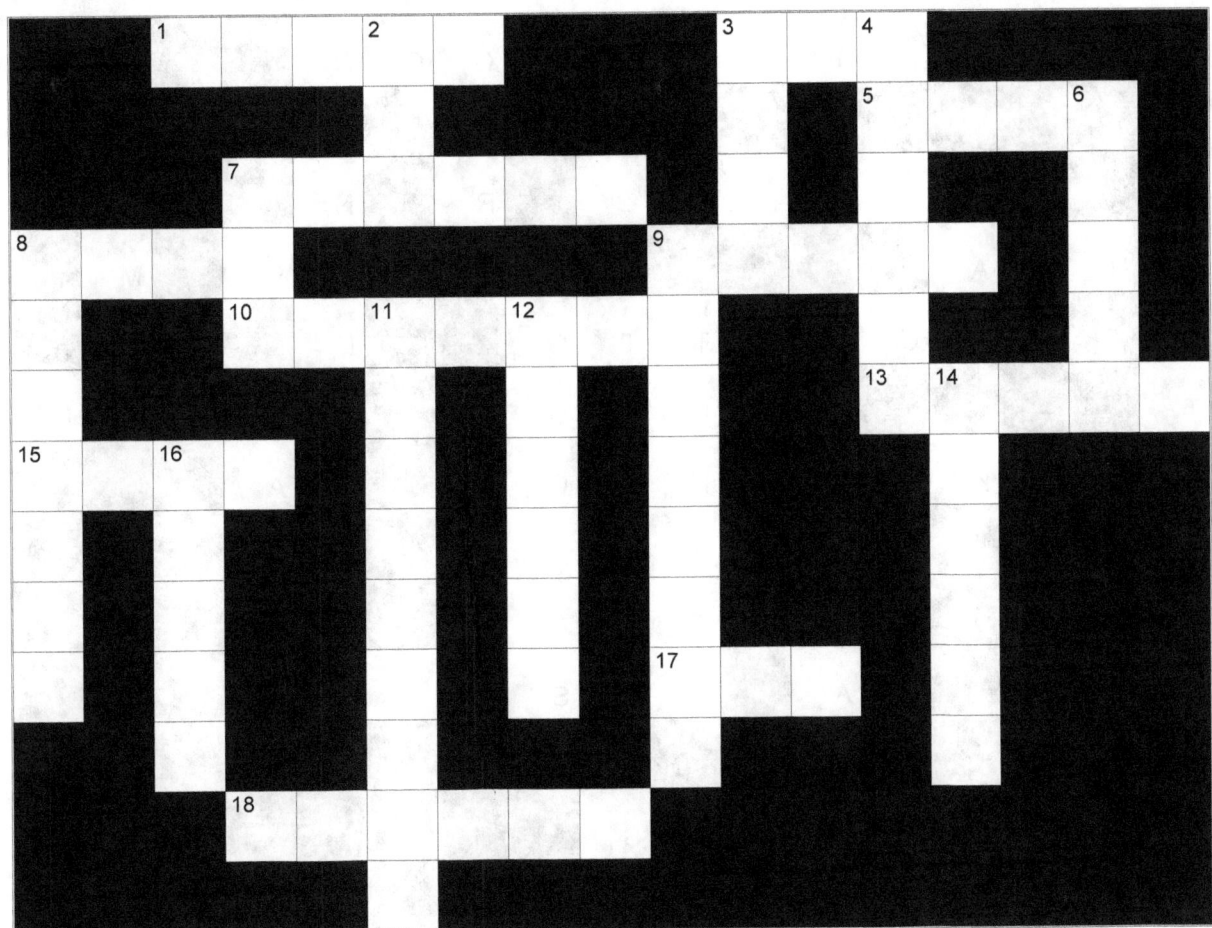

**Across**
1. 1818 is the estimated year of Douglass's ___.
3. Douglass attributed his good fortune to ___.
5. Taught Douglass some of the alphabet and spelling
7. Douglass considered it as a step towards freedom: ___ out
8. Douglass's wife
9. Served by the slaveholding religion
10. Child with slave mother and white father
13. Col. who owned the plantation where Douglass first lived
15. Murdered Douglass's wife's cousin
17. Number of cents Hugh Auld gave Douglass from his wages
18. Did not give slaves enough to eat: Master ___

**Down**
2. The Colonel used it to keep slaves out of the garden.
3. Cruel; gave severe punishments
4. Lloyd who protected Frederick from older boys
6. Shot by Gore
7. Was cursed in the Bible; slaves supposedly descended from him
8. Douglass's white father, clerk to Lloyd: Aaron ___
9. Name came from the book Lady of the Lake
11. Paper Douglass began reading in New York
12. Douglass copied letters on it to learn to write.
14. Killed two slaves, one with a hatchet
16. Slave breaker Douglass eventually beat

# Frederick Douglass Crossword 3 Answer Key

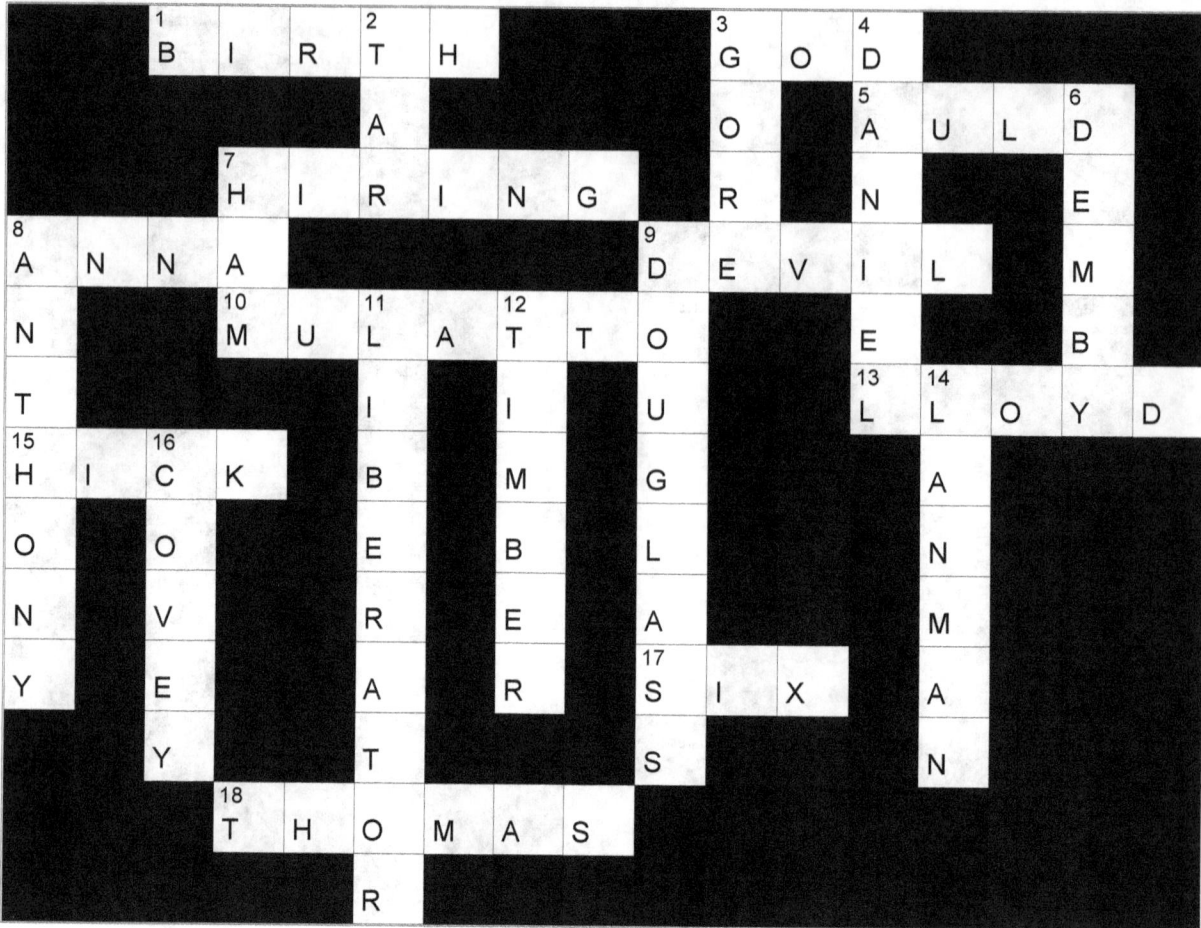

**Across**
1. 1818 is the estimated year of Douglass's ___.
3. Douglass attributed his good fortune to ___.
5. Taught Douglass some of the alphabet and spelling
7. Douglass considered it as a step towards freedom: ___ out
8. Douglass's wife
9. Served by the slaveholding religion
10. Child with slave mother and white father
13. Col. who owned the plantation where Douglass first lived
15. Murdered Douglass's wife's cousin
17. Number of cents Hugh Auld gave Douglass from his wages
18. Did not give slaves enough to eat: Master ___

**Down**
2. The Colonel used it to keep slaves out of the garden.
3. Cruel; gave severe punishments
4. Lloyd who protected Frederick from older boys
6. Shot by Gore
7. Was cursed in the Bible; slaves supposedly descended from him
8. Douglass's white father, clerk to Lloyd: Aaron ___
9. Name came from the book Lady of the Lake
11. Paper Douglass began reading in New York
12. Douglass copied letters on it to learn to write.
14. Killed two slaves, one with a hatchet
16. Slave breaker Douglass eventually beat

# Frederick Douglass Crossword 4

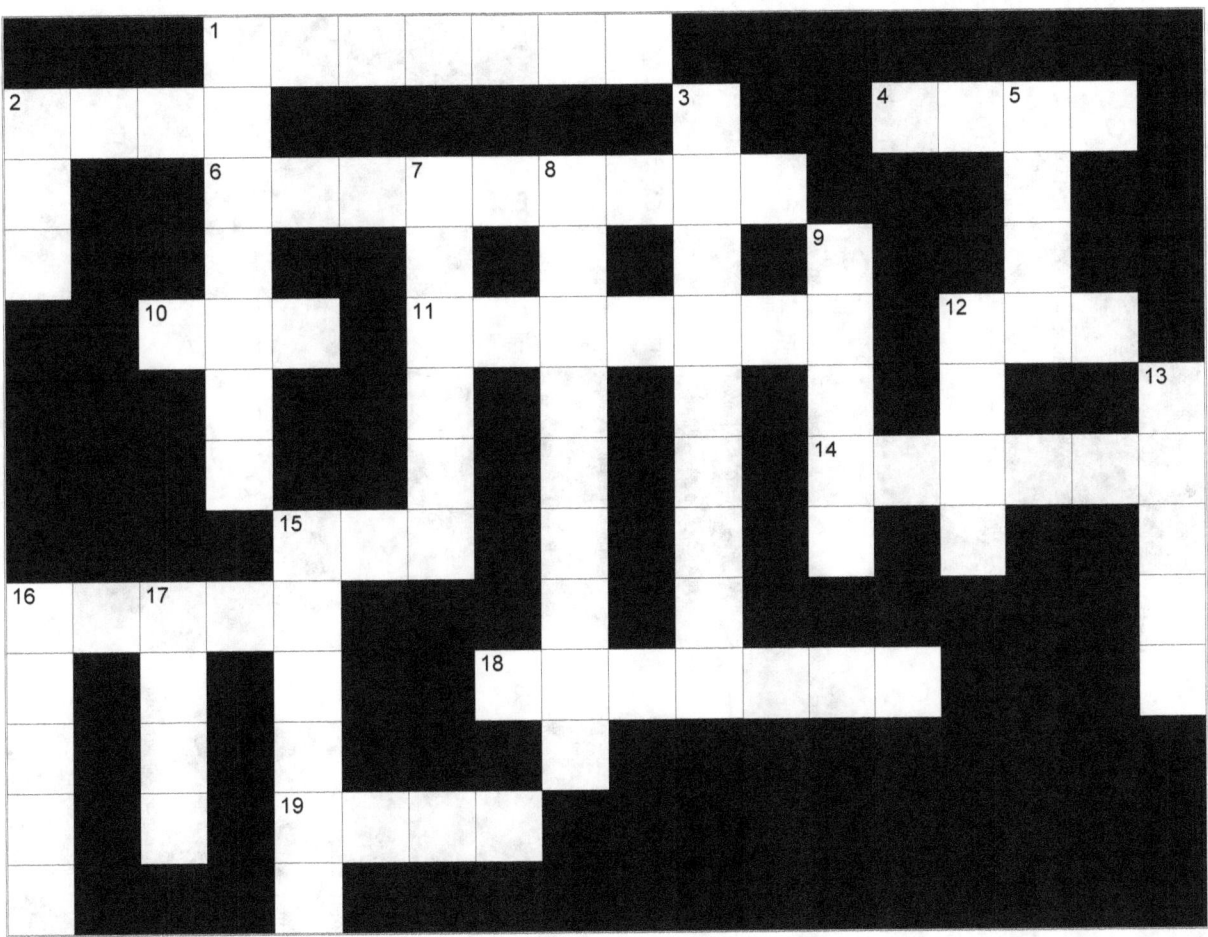

**Across**
1. Last name Douglass used in New York
2. Cruel; gave severe punishments
4. Shot and killed a slave with a musket: ___ Bondy
6. Location of anti-slavery meeting where Douglass first spoke
10. Number of cents Hugh Auld gave Douglass from his wages
11. Child with slave mother and white father
12. Was cursed in the Bible; slaves supposedly descended from him
14. This was easier to do from the city.
15. The Colonel used it to keep slaves out of the garden.
16. 1818 is the estimated year of Douglass's ___.
18. Douglass's mother
19. Taught Douglass some of the alphabet and spelling

**Down**
1. Slave who gave Douglass the root
2. Douglass attributed his good fortune to ___.
3. Month of Douglass's final escape
5. Douglass's wife
7. Douglass copied letters on it to learn to write.
8. Reading The ___ Orator helped Douglass argue against slavery.
9. Slave breaker Douglass eventually beat
12. Murdered Douglass's wife's cousin
13. Shot by Gore
15. Did not give slaves enough to eat: Master ___
16. Douglass traded it for reading lessons from white boys.
17. Supposed to keep slaves from being whipped: lucky ___

# Frederick Douglass Crossword 4 Answer Key

|   |   |   | ¹J | O | H | N | S | O | N |   |   |   |   |   |
|---|---|---|---|---|---|---|---|---|---|---|---|---|---|---|
| ²G | O | R | E |   |   |   |   | ³S |   | ⁴B | E | ⁵A | L |   |
| O |   | ⁶N | A | ⁷N | T | ⁸U | C | K | E | T |   | N |   |   |
| D |   | K |   | I |   | O |   | P |   |   | ⁹C |   | N |   |
|   | ¹⁰S | I | X | ¹¹M | U | L | A | T | T | O |   | ¹²H | A | M |
|   |   | N |   | B |   | U |   | E |   | V |   | I |   | ¹³D |
|   |   | S |   | E |   | M |   | M |   | ¹⁴E | S | C | A | P | E |
|   |   |   | ¹⁵T | A | R | B |   | B |   | Y |   | K |   | M |
| ¹⁶B | ¹⁷I | R | T | H |   | I |   | E |   |   |   |   |   | B |
| R | O |   | O |   | ¹⁸H | A | R | R | I | E | T |   |   | Y |
| E | O |   | M |   |   | N |   |   |   |   |   |   |   |   |
| A | T |   | ¹⁹A | U | L | D |   |   |   |   |   |   |   |   |
| D |   |   | S |   |   |   |   |   |   |   |   |   |   |   |

**Across**
1. Last name Douglass used in New York
2. Cruel; gave severe punishments
4. Shot and killed a slave with a musket: ___ Bondy
6. Location of anti-slavery meeting where Douglass first spoke
10. Number of cents Hugh Auld gave Douglass from his wages
11. Child with slave mother and white father
12. Was cursed in the Bible; slaves supposedly descended from him
14. This was easier to do from the city.
15. The Colonel used it to keep slaves out of the garden.
16. 1818 is the estimated year of Douglass's ___.
18. Douglass's mother
19. Taught Douglass some of the alphabet and spelling

**Down**
1. Slave who gave Douglass the root
2. Douglass attributed his good fortune to ___.
3. Month of Douglass's final escape
5. Douglass's wife
7. Douglass copied letters on it to learn to write.
8. Reading The ___ Orator helped Douglass argue against slavery.
9. Slave breaker Douglass eventually beat
12. Murdered Douglass's wife's cousin
13. Shot by Gore
15. Did not give slaves enough to eat: Master ___
16. Douglass traded it for reading lessons from white boys.
17. Supposed to keep slaves from being whipped: lucky ___

Frederick Douglass

| DOUGLASS | COVEY | BEAL | AULD | THOMAS |
|---|---|---|---|---|
| SEPTEMBER | GRANDMOTHER | ANNA | CAULKING | BIRTH |
| BALTIMORE | TAR | FREE SPACE | ROOT | SIX |
| GOD | BREAD | LANMAN | DEMBY | LIBERATOR |
| JOHNSON | DANIEL | HICK | ABOLITIONISTS | NANTUCKET |

Frederick Douglass

| FREDERICK | RUGGLES | HAM | LLOYD | TUCKAHOE |
|---|---|---|---|---|
| TIMBER | HARRIET | SEVEN | ESCAPE | MULATTO |
| ANTHONY | HIRING | FREE SPACE | GORE | BEDFORD |
| DEVIL | SINGING | JENKINS | RELIGIOUS | SHIPYARD |
| ARTFUL | NANTUCKET | ABOLITIONISTS | HICK | DANIEL |

Frederick Douglass

| COVEY | HICK | LLOYD | SEVEN | ANTHONY |
|---|---|---|---|---|
| DANIEL | ROOT | ARTFUL | TAR | CAULKING |
| SHIPYARD | ABOLITIONISTS | FREE SPACE | DOUGLASS | FREDERICK |
| NANTUCKET | AULD | RUGGLES | SINGING | SEPTEMBER |
| DEVIL | JOHNSON | SIX | TUCKAHOE | RELIGIOUS |

Frederick Douglass

| HIRING | MULATTO | GRANDMOTHER | ESCAPE | HAM |
|---|---|---|---|---|
| THOMAS | GOD | JENKINS | BEAL | BIRTH |
| TIMBER | COLUMBIAN | FREE SPACE | HARRIET | DEMBY |
| LIBERATOR | BALTIMORE | ANNA | LANMAN | GORE |
| BAILEY | RELIGIOUS | TUCKAHOE | SIX | JOHNSON |

Frederick Douglass

| BALTIMORE | SEPTEMBER | ANTHONY | HICK | BREAD |
|---|---|---|---|---|
| LANMAN | DANIEL | JOHNSON | GORE | BIRTH |
| DEMBY | TUCKAHOE | FREE SPACE | TIMBER | LIBERATOR |
| DOUGLASS | JENKINS | ANNA | DEVIL | COLUMBIAN |
| GOD | LLOYD | HIRING | BEAL | FREDERICK |

Frederick Douglass

| TAR | MULATTO | HARRIET | THOMAS | ARTFUL |
|---|---|---|---|---|
| ABOLITIONISTS | BAILEY | HAM | ROOT | ESCAPE |
| SHIPYARD | NANTUCKET | FREE SPACE | RELIGIOUS | SINGING |
| BEDFORD | RUGGLES | CAULKING | AULD | SIX |
| COVEY | FREDERICK | BEAL | HIRING | LLOYD |

Frederick Douglass

| BIRTH | ANTHONY | ABOLITIONISTS | HARRIET | SEVEN |
|---|---|---|---|---|
| GOD | THOMAS | GRANDMOTHER | CAULKING | FREDERICK |
| LLOYD | DEVIL | FREE SPACE | NANTUCKET | ESCAPE |
| JENKINS | DANIEL | AULD | DEMBY | BALTIMORE |
| HIRING | TIMBER | HICK | ANNA | SEPTEMBER |

Frederick Douglass

| BAILEY | SHIPYARD | ROOT | SIX | RELIGIOUS |
|---|---|---|---|---|
| BEAL | SINGING | TUCKAHOE | RUGGLES | HAM |
| MULATTO | LIBERATOR | FREE SPACE | ARTFUL | COVEY |
| LANMAN | GORE | COLUMBIAN | JOHNSON | BEDFORD |
| TAR | SEPTEMBER | ANNA | HICK | TIMBER |

Frederick Douglass

| TUCKAHOE | GRANDMOTHER | AULD | LIBERATOR | SIX |
|---|---|---|---|---|
| JOHNSON | FREDERICK | SEVEN | HAM | BEDFORD |
| GOD | RUGGLES | FREE SPACE | DOUGLASS | ROOT |
| CAULKING | DEMBY | DEVIL | SHIPYARD | SEPTEMBER |
| ESCAPE | DANIEL | MULATTO | ANNA | TIMBER |

Frederick Douglass

| HICK | TAR | BALTIMORE | NANTUCKET | COVEY |
|---|---|---|---|---|
| THOMAS | ARTFUL | HIRING | BEAL | BREAD |
| LANMAN | ANTHONY | FREE SPACE | HARRIET | LLOYD |
| SINGING | GORE | BAILEY | COLUMBIAN | JENKINS |
| ABOLITIONISTS | TIMBER | ANNA | MULATTO | DANIEL |

Frederick Douglass

| HIRING | DEMBY | ROOT | GORE | CAULKING |
|---|---|---|---|---|
| LANMAN | LIBERATOR | TAR | BREAD | LLOYD |
| DEVIL | ABOLITIONISTS | FREE SPACE | RELIGIOUS | AULD |
| SINGING | ESCAPE | GRANDMOTHER | BALTIMORE | THOMAS |
| JENKINS | NANTUCKET | COLUMBIAN | TIMBER | JOHNSON |

Frederick Douglass

| SHIPYARD | ARTFUL | BIRTH | SEPTEMBER | SIX |
|---|---|---|---|---|
| GOD | DOUGLASS | ANNA | FREDERICK | BEAL |
| MULATTO | BEDFORD | FREE SPACE | SEVEN | ANTHONY |
| COVEY | HICK | BAILEY | HARRIET | RUGGLES |
| DANIEL | JOHNSON | TIMBER | COLUMBIAN | NANTUCKET |

Frederick Douglass

| GOD | LANMAN | DOUGLASS | BEDFORD | DEVIL |
|---|---|---|---|---|
| CAULKING | ANNA | JENKINS | DEMBY | BREAD |
| BEAL | LIBERATOR | FREE SPACE | TIMBER | GRANDMOTHER |
| ESCAPE | LLOYD | TAR | BAILEY | GORE |
| THOMAS | MULATTO | SEVEN | RELIGIOUS | HIRING |

Frederick Douglass

| SIX | HARRIET | ANTHONY | ABOLITIONISTS | BALTIMORE |
|---|---|---|---|---|
| JOHNSON | ROOT | COVEY | HICK | BIRTH |
| ARTFUL | SINGING | FREE SPACE | NANTUCKET | FREDERICK |
| DANIEL | COLUMBIAN | SHIPYARD | SEPTEMBER | TUCKAHOE |
| AULD | HIRING | RELIGIOUS | SEVEN | MULATTO |

Frederick Douglass

| JOHNSON | DEMBY | HIRING | HARRIET | BREAD |
|---|---|---|---|---|
| SEVEN | TIMBER | HICK | COVEY | ABOLITIONISTS |
| JENKINS | DANIEL | FREE SPACE | RUGGLES | ROOT |
| THOMAS | SINGING | CAULKING | BEAL | BEDFORD |
| LANMAN | NANTUCKET | ARTFUL | GORE | FREDERICK |

Frederick Douglass

| ANTHONY | RELIGIOUS | SEPTEMBER | GRANDMOTHER | MULATTO |
|---|---|---|---|---|
| LLOYD | BIRTH | DEVIL | ESCAPE | BALTIMORE |
| HAM | SIX | FREE SPACE | TAR | COLUMBIAN |
| GOD | ANNA | DOUGLASS | TUCKAHOE | BAILEY |
| SHIPYARD | FREDERICK | GORE | ARTFUL | NANTUCKET |

## Frederick Douglass

| SINGING | LLOYD | BIRTH | BEDFORD | HAM |
|---------|-------|-------|---------|-----|
| MULATTO | COVEY | AULD | BREAD | DEMBY |
| HIRING | FREDERICK | FREE SPACE | COLUMBIAN | SEVEN |
| CAULKING | LANMAN | BEAL | JENKINS | ESCAPE |
| ARTFUL | DEVIL | TUCKAHOE | ROOT | HICK |

## Frederick Douglass

| BAILEY | ANNA | TIMBER | ANTHONY | NANTUCKET |
|--------|------|--------|---------|-----------|
| LIBERATOR | RUGGLES | SHIPYARD | TAR | BALTIMORE |
| HARRIET | THOMAS | FREE SPACE | GORE | GOD |
| RELIGIOUS | SIX | JOHNSON | DOUGLASS | SEPTEMBER |
| GRANDMOTHER | HICK | ROOT | TUCKAHOE | DEVIL |

## Frederick Douglass

| | | | | |
|---|---|---|---|---|
| HIRING | MULATTO | HICK | THOMAS | DANIEL |
| BAILEY | SHIPYARD | BEDFORD | FREDERICK | BIRTH |
| DEMBY | GORE | FREE SPACE | SINGING | GRANDMOTHER |
| SEVEN | LANMAN | BREAD | LIBERATOR | JENKINS |
| BALTIMORE | AULD | JOHNSON | SIX | RELIGIOUS |

## Frederick Douglass

| | | | | |
|---|---|---|---|---|
| BEAL | LLOYD | TIMBER | COLUMBIAN | CAULKING |
| HAM | ABOLITIONISTS | HARRIET | ANNA | COVEY |
| SEPTEMBER | ESCAPE | FREE SPACE | RUGGLES | NANTUCKET |
| DEVIL | ANTHONY | ARTFUL | DOUGLASS | TUCKAHOE |
| ROOT | RELIGIOUS | SIX | JOHNSON | AULD |

Frederick Douglass

| BAILEY | SEVEN | ANTHONY | LIBERATOR | HIRING |
|---|---|---|---|---|
| HICK | LANMAN | THOMAS | ESCAPE | BIRTH |
| NANTUCKET | FREDERICK | FREE SPACE | JOHNSON | COLUMBIAN |
| BEAL | CAULKING | DOUGLASS | BEDFORD | SHIPYARD |
| HARRIET | RELIGIOUS | GORE | ARTFUL | TAR |

Frederick Douglass

| RUGGLES | TUCKAHOE | DEVIL | LLOYD | BREAD |
|---|---|---|---|---|
| DANIEL | ANNA | COVEY | DEMBY | ROOT |
| BALTIMORE | SINGING | FREE SPACE | AULD | GOD |
| HAM | TIMBER | GRANDMOTHER | ABOLITIONISTS | SIX |
| JENKINS | TAR | ARTFUL | GORE | RELIGIOUS |

Frederick Douglass

| BEAL | BREAD | GRANDMOTHER | BIRTH | DEMBY |
|---|---|---|---|---|
| SEVEN | CAULKING | HICK | TIMBER | SEPTEMBER |
| JENKINS | SINGING | FREE SPACE | ARTFUL | ESCAPE |
| LIBERATOR | LANMAN | SHIPYARD | DEVIL | COVEY |
| DOUGLASS | JOHNSON | SIX | DANIEL | ABOLITIONISTS |

Frederick Douglass

| BAILEY | RUGGLES | NANTUCKET | HARRIET | FREDERICK |
|---|---|---|---|---|
| TAR | ANNA | ROOT | ANTHONY | HAM |
| HIRING | TUCKAHOE | FREE SPACE | COLUMBIAN | AULD |
| LLOYD | GOD | MULATTO | GORE | RELIGIOUS |
| BALTIMORE | ABOLITIONISTS | DANIEL | SIX | JOHNSON |

## Frederick Douglass

| SEPTEMBER | TIMBER | JOHNSON | GRANDMOTHER | JENKINS |
|---|---|---|---|---|
| DOUGLASS | GORE | ABOLITIONISTS | THOMAS | CAULKING |
| BEAL | TUCKAHOE | FREE SPACE | RUGGLES | DEVIL |
| LIBERATOR | FREDERICK | HIRING | NANTUCKET | BALTIMORE |
| GOD | COVEY | AULD | DANIEL | HICK |

## Frederick Douglass

| HAM | LLOYD | ESCAPE | MULATTO | SINGING |
|---|---|---|---|---|
| SIX | RELIGIOUS | SHIPYARD | ROOT | SEVEN |
| COLUMBIAN | BAILEY | FREE SPACE | TAR | BIRTH |
| ARTFUL | BEDFORD | ANTHONY | DEMBY | HARRIET |
| BREAD | HICK | DANIEL | AULD | COVEY |

Frederick Douglass

| SHIPYARD | GRANDMOTHER | TUCKAHOE | SINGING | GORE |
|---|---|---|---|---|
| AULD | DANIEL | JENKINS | TIMBER | BAILEY |
| HARRIET | BREAD | FREE SPACE | HIRING | MULATTO |
| ANNA | COLUMBIAN | ROOT | BALTIMORE | LLOYD |
| DEMBY | CAULKING | ARTFUL | NANTUCKET | GOD |

Frederick Douglass

| RELIGIOUS | LANMAN | COVEY | SEPTEMBER | THOMAS |
|---|---|---|---|---|
| ABOLITIONISTS | DOUGLASS | JOHNSON | HICK | BIRTH |
| TAR | DEVIL | FREE SPACE | ESCAPE | SIX |
| LIBERATOR | HAM | FREDERICK | SEVEN | BEDFORD |
| ANTHONY | GOD | NANTUCKET | ARTFUL | CAULKING |

Frederick Douglass

| LANMAN | TAR | MULATTO | HAM | HIRING |
|--------|-----|---------|-----|--------|
| JENKINS | SEVEN | LIBERATOR | BEAL | DEVIL |
| AULD | BALTIMORE | FREE SPACE | BEDFORD | SHIPYARD |
| DEMBY | GOD | ABOLITIONISTS | HICK | BAILEY |
| RUGGLES | GRANDMOTHER | SIX | JOHNSON | SINGING |

Frederick Douglass

| TUCKAHOE | BIRTH | BREAD | HARRIET | ANNA |
|----------|-------|-------|---------|------|
| SEPTEMBER | ROOT | ARTFUL | ANTHONY | RELIGIOUS |
| NANTUCKET | LLOYD | FREE SPACE | DANIEL | FREDERICK |
| DOUGLASS | CAULKING | THOMAS | COVEY | COLUMBIAN |
| ESCAPE | SINGING | JOHNSON | SIX | GRANDMOTHER |

Frederick Douglass

| ROOT | COLUMBIAN | SEPTEMBER | HICK | DEMBY |
|---|---|---|---|---|
| SHIPYARD | LLOYD | MULATTO | BEAL | BIRTH |
| HIRING | BALTIMORE | FREE SPACE | ANNA | BREAD |
| LIBERATOR | DOUGLASS | THOMAS | GOD | BEDFORD |
| RELIGIOUS | TIMBER | AULD | TUCKAHOE | DANIEL |

Frederick Douglass

| CAULKING | ANTHONY | ABOLITIONISTS | FREDERICK | ARTFUL |
|---|---|---|---|---|
| GRANDMOTHER | NANTUCKET | DEVIL | SINGING | JENKINS |
| HARRIET | SEVEN | FREE SPACE | GORE | HAM |
| RUGGLES | BAILEY | LANMAN | ESCAPE | COVEY |
| TAR | DANIEL | TUCKAHOE | AULD | TIMBER |

# Frederick Douglass Vocabulary Word List

| No. | Word | Clue/Definition |
|---|---|---|
| 1. | ABHORRENCE | Intense disapproval or dislike |
| 2. | AGITATED | Anxious; nervous |
| 3. | ANNIHILATE | Destroy |
| 4. | APPALLED | Shocked; horrified |
| 5. | ARDENTLY | Enthusiastically |
| 6. | AUTHENTIC | Genuine; real |
| 7. | AVAILED | Made useful; helped |
| 8. | BENEVOLENCE | Kindness; compassion; good will |
| 9. | CENSURED | Severely criticized |
| 10. | COMMENSURATE | Equal |
| 11. | CONJECTURE | Guessing |
| 12. | CONSUMMATE | Complete |
| 13. | DEFICIENCY | Lack; shortage |
| 14. | DEFILED | Having one's good name ruined |
| 15. | DENUNCIATION | Condemnation; criticism |
| 16. | DEPRAVITY | Evil; wickedness |
| 17. | DESOLATE | Deserted; uninhabited |
| 18. | DESTITUTE | Totally lacking |
| 19. | DETESTATION | Hatred; loathing |
| 20. | EMANCIPATION | Setting free |
| 21. | EXCULPATE | To free from blame |
| 22. | EXHORTED | Urged; insisted |
| 23. | IMBIBED | Took into the mind; absorbed |
| 24. | IMBUE | Fill |
| 25. | IMMUTABLE | Not changeable |
| 26. | IMPERTINENT | Rude; disrespectful |
| 27. | IMPUDENCE | Rude behavior |
| 28. | IMPUTATIONS | Accusations |
| 29. | INCOHERENT | Rambling; confused; disjointed |
| 30. | INFIDEL | A person without belief in the religion of the writer |
| 31. | MANIFESTATION | Expression; revelation; display |
| 32. | MAXIM | Saying; a truth |
| 33. | MYRIADS | Huge numbers |
| 34. | OBDURATE | Stubborn |
| 35. | ODIOUSNESS | Being full of hatred |
| 36. | PERDITION | State of everlasting punishment; hell |
| 37. | PERNICIOUS | Destructive; harmful |
| 38. | PERPLEXING | Puzzling; confusing |
| 39. | PROFLIGATE | Wasteful; extremely extravagant |
| 40. | PROVIDENCE | Care or guardianship exercised by a deity |
| 41. | QUAILED | Drew back in fear |
| 42. | RAPTURE | Delight; joy |
| 43. | RETALIATION | Revenge; getting even |
| 44. | SAGACITY | Wisdom |
| 45. | SCANTY | Less than is needed |
| 46. | SCATHING | Scornful; mocking |
| 47. | SUNDERED | Separated |
| 48. | VIGILANCE | Care; watchfulness |
| 49. | VINDICATION | Support; justification |

Frederick Douglass Vocabulary Fill In The Blanks 1

_____  1. Genuine; real
_____  2. Puzzling; confusing
_____  3. Intense disapproval or dislike
_____  4. Anxious; nervous
_____  5. Guessing
_____  6. Shocked; horrified
_____  7. Revenge; getting even
_____  8. Expression; revelation; display
_____  9. Saying; a truth
_____  10. Destructive; harmful
_____  11. State of everlasting punishment; hell
_____  12. A person without belief in the religion of the writer
_____  13. Lack; shortage
_____  14. Accusations
_____  15. Rambling; confused; disjointed
_____  16. Separated
_____  17. Made useful; helped
_____  18. Severely criticized
_____  19. Care; watchfulness
_____  20. Being full of hatred

Frederick Douglass Vocabulary Fill In The Blanks 1 Answer Key

| | |
|---|---|
| AUTHENTIC | 1. Genuine; real |
| PERPLEXING | 2. Puzzling; confusing |
| ABHORRENCE | 3. Intense disapproval or dislike |
| AGITATED | 4. Anxious; nervous |
| CONJECTURE | 5. Guessing |
| APPALLED | 6. Shocked; horrified |
| RETALIATION | 7. Revenge; getting even |
| MANIFESTATION | 8. Expression; revelation; display |
| MAXIM | 9. Saying; a truth |
| PERNICIOUS | 10. Destructive; harmful |
| PERDITION | 11. State of everlasting punishment; hell |
| INFIDEL | 12. A person without belief in the religion of the writer |
| DEFICIENCY | 13. Lack; shortage |
| IMPUTATIONS | 14. Accusations |
| INCOHERENT | 15. Rambling; confused; disjointed |
| SUNDERED | 16. Separated |
| AVAILED | 17. Made useful; helped |
| CENSURED | 18. Severely criticized |
| VIGILANCE | 19. Care; watchfulness |
| ODIOUSNESS | 20. Being full of hatred |

Frederick Douglass Vocabulary Fill In The Blanks 2

_____  1. Stubborn

_____  2. Guessing

_____  3. Delight; joy

_____  4. Destroy

_____  5. Rambling; confused; disjointed

_____  6. Made useful; helped

_____  7. Separated

_____  8. Not changeable

_____  9. Destructive; harmful

_____  10. Took into the mind; absorbed

_____  11. Less than is needed

_____  12. Enthusiastically

_____  13. Hatred; loathing

_____  14. Anxious; nervous

_____  15. Puzzling; confusing

_____  16. Saying; a truth

_____  17. Kindness; compassion; good will

_____  18. A person without belief in the religion of the writer

_____  19. Lack; shortage

_____  20. Deserted; uninhabited

Frederick Douglass Vocabulary Fill In The Blanks 2 Answer Key

|  |  |
|---|---|
| OBDURATE | 1. Stubborn |
| CONJECTURE | 2. Guessing |
| RAPTURE | 3. Delight; joy |
| ANNIHILATE | 4. Destroy |
| INCOHERENT | 5. Rambling; confused; disjointed |
| AVAILED | 6. Made useful; helped |
| SUNDERED | 7. Separated |
| IMMUTABLE | 8. Not changeable |
| PERNICIOUS | 9. Destructive; harmful |
| IMBIBED | 10. Took into the mind; absorbed |
| SCANTY | 11. Less than is needed |
| ARDENTLY | 12. Enthusiastically |
| DETESTATION | 13. Hatred; loathing |
| AGITATED | 14. Anxious; nervous |
| PERPLEXING | 15. Puzzling; confusing |
| MAXIM | 16. Saying; a truth |
| BENEVOLENCE | 17. Kindness; compassion; good will |
| INFIDEL | 18. A person without belief in the religion of the writer |
| DEFICIENCY | 19. Lack; shortage |
| DESOLATE | 20. Deserted; uninhabited |

# Frederick Douglass Vocabulary Fill In The Blanks 3

_____   1. Rude; disrespectful

_____   2. Severely criticized

_____   3. Fill

_____   4. Genuine; real

_____   5. To free from blame

_____   6. A person without belief in the religion of the writer

_____   7. Setting free

_____   8. Condemnation; criticism

_____   9. Destructive; harmful

_____   10. Rude behavior

_____   11. State of everlasting punishment; hell

_____   12. Hatred; loathing

_____   13. Lack; shortage

_____   14. Equal

_____   15. Anxious; nervous

_____   16. Saying; a truth

_____   17. Support; justification

_____   18. Stubborn

_____   19. Less than is needed

_____   20. Scornful; mocking

Frederick Douglass Vocabulary Fill In The Blanks 3 Answer Key

| | |
|---|---|
| IMPERTINENT | 1. Rude; disrespectful |
| CENSURED | 2. Severely criticized |
| IMBUE | 3. Fill |
| AUTHENTIC | 4. Genuine; real |
| EXCULPATE | 5. To free from blame |
| INFIDEL | 6. A person without belief in the religion of the writer |
| EMANCIPATION | 7. Setting free |
| DENUNCIATION | 8. Condemnation; criticism |
| PERNICIOUS | 9. Destructive; harmful |
| IMPUDENCE | 10. Rude behavior |
| PERDITION | 11. State of everlasting punishment; hell |
| DETESTATION | 12. Hatred; loathing |
| DEFICIENCY | 13. Lack; shortage |
| COMMENSURATE | 14. Equal |
| AGITATED | 15. Anxious; nervous |
| MAXIM | 16. Saying; a truth |
| VINDICATION | 17. Support; justification |
| OBDURATE | 18. Stubborn |
| SCANTY | 19. Less than is needed |
| SCATHING | 20. Scornful; mocking |

Frederick Douglass Vocabulary Fill In The Blanks 4

_____  1. Huge numbers

_____  2. Equal

_____  3. Rambling; confused; disjointed

_____  4. Accusations

_____  5. Being full of hatred

_____  6. Less than is needed

_____  7. Lack; shortage

_____  8. Setting free

_____  9. Shocked; horrified

_____  10. Revenge; getting even

_____  11. Saying; a truth

_____  12. A person without belief in the religion of the writer

_____  13. Intense disapproval or dislike

_____  14. State of everlasting punishment; hell

_____  15. Genuine; real

_____  16. Condemnation; criticism

_____  17. Having one's good name ruined

_____  18. Separated

_____  19. Wasteful; extremely extravagant

_____  20. Severely criticized

Frederick Douglass Vocabulary Fill In The Blanks 4 Answer Key

| | |
|---|---|
| MYRIADS | 1. Huge numbers |
| COMMENSURATE | 2. Equal |
| INCOHERENT | 3. Rambling; confused; disjointed |
| IMPUTATIONS | 4. Accusations |
| ODIOUSNESS | 5. Being full of hatred |
| SCANTY | 6. Less than is needed |
| DEFICIENCY | 7. Lack; shortage |
| EMANCIPATION | 8. Setting free |
| APPALLED | 9. Shocked; horrified |
| RETALIATION | 10. Revenge; getting even |
| MAXIM | 11. Saying; a truth |
| INFIDEL | 12. A person without belief in the religion of the writer |
| ABHORRENCE | 13. Intense disapproval or dislike |
| PERDITION | 14. State of everlasting punishment; hell |
| AUTHENTIC | 15. Genuine; real |
| DENUNCIATION | 16. Condemnation; criticism |
| DEFILED | 17. Having one's good name ruined |
| SUNDERED | 18. Separated |
| PROFLIGATE | 19. Wasteful; extremely extravagant |
| CENSURED | 20. Severely criticized |

Frederick Douglass Vocabulary Matching 1

___ 1. PROFLIGATE          A. Support; justification
___ 2. VIGILANCE           B. Fill
___ 3. MAXIM               C. Stubborn
___ 4. PROVIDENCE          D. Expression; revelation; display
___ 5. VINDICATION         E. Saying; a truth
___ 6. ARDENTLY            F. Made useful; helped
___ 7. EXCULPATE           G. Huge numbers
___ 8. PERNICIOUS          H. Complete
___ 9. APPALLED            I. State of everlasting punishment; hell
___10. MYRIADS             J. A person without belief in the religion of the writer
___11. INFIDEL             K. To free from blame
___12. CENSURED            L. Having one's good name ruined
___13. SCATHING            M. Delight; joy
___14. AVAILED             N. Puzzling; confusing
___15. PERDITION           O. Deserted; uninhabited
___16. EMANCIPATION        P. Care; watchfulness
___17. OBDURATE            Q. Destructive; harmful
___18. IMBUE               R. Less than is needed
___19. DESOLATE            S. Enthusiastically
___20. SCANTY              T. Shocked; horrified
___21. RAPTURE             U. Care or guardianship exercised by a deity
___22. MANIFESTATION       V. Setting free
___23. PERPLEXING          W. Scornful; mocking
___24. CONSUMMATE          X. Wasteful; extremely extravagant
___25. DEFILED             Y. Severely criticized

Frederick Douglass Vocabulary Matching 1 Answer Key

| | |
|---|---|
| X - 1. PROFLIGATE | A. Support; justification |
| P - 2. VIGILANCE | B. Fill |
| E - 3. MAXIM | C. Stubborn |
| U - 4. PROVIDENCE | D. Expression; revelation; display |
| A - 5. VINDICATION | E. Saying; a truth |
| S - 6. ARDENTLY | F. Made useful; helped |
| K - 7. EXCULPATE | G. Huge numbers |
| Q - 8. PERNICIOUS | H. Complete |
| T - 9. APPALLED | I. State of everlasting punishment; hell |
| G - 10. MYRIADS | J. A person without belief in the religion of the writer |
| J - 11. INFIDEL | K. To free from blame |
| Y - 12. CENSURED | L. Having one's good name ruined |
| W - 13. SCATHING | M. Delight; joy |
| F - 14. AVAILED | N. Puzzling; confusing |
| I - 15. PERDITION | O. Deserted; uninhabited |
| V - 16. EMANCIPATION | P. Care; watchfulness |
| C - 17. OBDURATE | Q. Destructive; harmful |
| B - 18. IMBUE | R. Less than is needed |
| O - 19. DESOLATE | S. Enthusiastically |
| R - 20. SCANTY | T. Shocked; horrified |
| M - 21. RAPTURE | U. Care or guardianship exercised by a deity |
| D - 22. MANIFESTATION | V. Setting free |
| N - 23. PERPLEXING | W. Scornful; mocking |
| H - 24. CONSUMMATE | X. Wasteful; extremely extravagant |
| L - 25. DEFILED | Y. Severely criticized |

Frederick Douglass Vocabulary Matching 2

___ 1. APPALLED         A. Deserted; uninhabited
___ 2. MYRIADS          B. State of everlasting punishment; hell
___ 3. OBDURATE         C. Condemnation; criticism
___ 4. IMPUTATIONS      D. Stubborn
___ 5. MAXIM            E. Huge numbers
___ 6. DEFICIENCY       F. Lack; shortage
___ 7. AGITATED         G. Fill
___ 8. SCATHING         H. Intense disapproval or dislike
___ 9. EXCULPATE        I. Genuine; real
___10. DENUNCIATION     J. Less than is needed
___11. IMPUDENCE        K. Care; watchfulness
___12. DEFILED          L. Accusations
___13. AUTHENTIC        M. Made useful; helped
___14. RAPTURE          N. Having one's good name ruined
___15. AVAILED          O. Not changeable
___16. PERDITION        P. Expression; revelation; display
___17. IMBUE            Q. Rude behavior
___18. MANIFESTATION    R. Being full of hatred
___19. ABHORRENCE       S. Care or guardianship exercised by a deity
___20. PROVIDENCE       T. Scornful; mocking
___21. IMMUTABLE        U. Saying; a truth
___22. DESOLATE         V. Anxious; nervous
___23. ODIOUSNESS       W. Shocked; horrified
___24. VIGILANCE        X. Delight; joy
___25. SCANTY           Y. To free from blame

Frederick Douglass Vocabulary Matching 2 Answer Key

| | |
|---|---|
| W - 1. APPALLED | A. Deserted; uninhabited |
| E - 2. MYRIADS | B. State of everlasting punishment; hell |
| D - 3. OBDURATE | C. Condemnation; criticism |
| L - 4. IMPUTATIONS | D. Stubborn |
| U - 5. MAXIM | E. Huge numbers |
| F - 6. DEFICIENCY | F. Lack; shortage |
| V - 7. AGITATED | G. Fill |
| T - 8. SCATHING | H. Intense disapproval or dislike |
| Y - 9. EXCULPATE | I. Genuine; real |
| C - 10. DENUNCIATION | J. Less than is needed |
| Q - 11. IMPUDENCE | K. Care; watchfulness |
| N - 12. DEFILED | L. Accusations |
| I - 13. AUTHENTIC | M. Made useful; helped |
| X - 14. RAPTURE | N. Having one's good name ruined |
| M - 15. AVAILED | O. Not changeable |
| B - 16. PERDITION | P. Expression; revelation; display |
| G - 17. IMBUE | Q. Rude behavior |
| P - 18. MANIFESTATION | R. Being full of hatred |
| H - 19. ABHORRENCE | S. Care or guardianship exercised by a deity |
| S - 20. PROVIDENCE | T. Scornful; mocking |
| O - 21. IMMUTABLE | U. Saying; a truth |
| A - 22. DESOLATE | V. Anxious; nervous |
| R - 23. ODIOUSNESS | W. Shocked; horrified |
| K - 24. VIGILANCE | X. Delight; joy |
| J - 25. SCANTY | Y. To free from blame |

Frederick Douglass Vocabulary Matching 3

___ 1. IMPUDENCE          A. Care or guardianship exercised by a deity
___ 2. PERNICIOUS         B. To free from blame
___ 3. RETALIATION        C. Equal
___ 4. ABHORRENCE         D. Evil; wickedness
___ 5. AUTHENTIC          E. Intense disapproval or dislike
___ 6. DESTITUTE          F. Being full of hatred
___ 7. AVAILED            G. Totally lacking
___ 8. DETESTATION        H. Complete
___ 9. DESOLATE           I. Anxious; nervous
___10. EMANCIPATION       J. Puzzling; confusing
___11. DENUNCIATION       K. Rude behavior
___12. BENEVOLENCE        L. Fill
___13. DEPRAVITY          M. Genuine; real
___14. IMBUE              N. Hatred; loathing
___15. EXCULPATE          O. Setting free
___16. VINDICATION        P. Deserted; uninhabited
___17. CONSUMMATE         Q. Having one's good name ruined
___18. DEFILED            R. Kindness; compassion; good will
___19. COMMENSURATE       S. Revenge; getting even
___20. ODIOUSNESS         T. Took into the mind; absorbed
___21. PERPLEXING         U. Condemnation; criticism
___22. SCANTY             V. Less than is needed
___23. IMBIBED            W. Destructive; harmful
___24. PROVIDENCE         X. Made useful; helped
___25. AGITATED           Y. Support; justification

Frederick Douglass Vocabulary Matching 3 Answer Key

| | |
|---|---|
| K - 1. IMPUDENCE | A. Care or guardianship exercised by a deity |
| W - 2. PERNICIOUS | B. To free from blame |
| S - 3. RETALIATION | C. Equal |
| E - 4. ABHORRENCE | D. Evil; wickedness |
| M - 5. AUTHENTIC | E. Intense disapproval or dislike |
| G - 6. DESTITUTE | F. Being full of hatred |
| X - 7. AVAILED | G. Totally lacking |
| N - 8. DETESTATION | H. Complete |
| P - 9. DESOLATE | I. Anxious; nervous |
| O - 10. EMANCIPATION | J. Puzzling; confusing |
| U - 11. DENUNCIATION | K. Rude behavior |
| R - 12. BENEVOLENCE | L. Fill |
| D - 13. DEPRAVITY | M. Genuine; real |
| L - 14. IMBUE | N. Hatred; loathing |
| B - 15. EXCULPATE | O. Setting free |
| Y - 16. VINDICATION | P. Deserted; uninhabited |
| H - 17. CONSUMMATE | Q. Having one's good name ruined |
| Q - 18. DEFILED | R. Kindness; compassion; good will |
| C - 19. COMMENSURATE | S. Revenge; getting even |
| F - 20. ODIOUSNESS | T. Took into the mind; absorbed |
| J - 21. PERPLEXING | U. Condemnation; criticism |
| V - 22. SCANTY | V. Less than is needed |
| T - 23. IMBIBED | W. Destructive; harmful |
| A - 24. PROVIDENCE | X. Made useful; helped |
| I - 25. AGITATED | Y. Support; justification |

Frederick Douglass Vocabulary Matching 4

___ 1. EMANCIPATION         A. To free from blame
___ 2. IMPUTATIONS           B. Enthusiastically
___ 3. CENSURED              C. Equal
___ 4. COMMENSURATE          D. Care or guardianship exercised by a deity
___ 5. SCATHING              E. Severely criticized
___ 6. DENUNCIATION          F. Separated
___ 7. DEFICIENCY            G. Fill
___ 8. IMPUDENCE             H. Accusations
___ 9. BENEVOLENCE           I. Condemnation; criticism
___10. SUNDERED              J. Took into the mind; absorbed
___11. IMBUE                 K. Rude; disrespectful
___12. AVAILED               L. Not changeable
___13. AUTHENTIC             M. Destructive; harmful
___14. ARDENTLY              N. Genuine; real
___15. EXCULPATE             O. Made useful; helped
___16. QUAILED               P. Kindness; compassion; good will
___17. PERDITION             Q. Drew back in fear
___18. PERNICIOUS            R. Setting free
___19. MYRIADS               S. Complete
___20. IMPERTINENT           T. Revenge; getting even
___21. CONSUMMATE            U. Scornful; mocking
___22. RETALIATION           V. Rude behavior
___23. IMBIBED               W. Lack; shortage
___24. PROVIDENCE            X. Huge numbers
___25. IMMUTABLE             Y. State of everlasting punishment; hell

Frederick Douglass Vocabulary Matching 4 Answer Key

| | | |
|---|---|---|
| R - 1. EMANCIPATION | | A. To free from blame |
| H - 2. IMPUTATIONS | | B. Enthusiastically |
| E - 3. CENSURED | | C. Equal |
| C - 4. COMMENSURATE | | D. Care or guardianship exercised by a deity |
| U - 5. SCATHING | | E. Severely criticized |
| I - 6. DENUNCIATION | | F. Separated |
| W - 7. DEFICIENCY | | G. Fill |
| V - 8. IMPUDENCE | | H. Accusations |
| P - 9. BENEVOLENCE | | I. Condemnation; criticism |
| F - 10. SUNDERED | | J. Took into the mind; absorbed |
| G - 11. IMBUE | | K. Rude; disrespectful |
| O - 12. AVAILED | | L. Not changeable |
| N - 13. AUTHENTIC | | M. Destructive; harmful |
| B - 14. ARDENTLY | | N. Genuine; real |
| A - 15. EXCULPATE | | O. Made useful; helped |
| Q - 16. QUAILED | | P. Kindness; compassion; good will |
| Y - 17. PERDITION | | Q. Drew back in fear |
| M - 18. PERNICIOUS | | R. Setting free |
| X - 19. MYRIADS | | S. Complete |
| K - 20. IMPERTINENT | | T. Revenge; getting even |
| S - 21. CONSUMMATE | | U. Scornful; mocking |
| T - 22. RETALIATION | | V. Rude behavior |
| J - 23. IMBIBED | | W. Lack; shortage |
| D - 24. PROVIDENCE | | X. Huge numbers |
| L - 25. IMMUTABLE | | Y. State of everlasting punishment; hell |

Frederick Douglass Vocabulary Magic Squares 1

Match the definition with the vocabulary word. Put your answers in the magic squares below. When your answers are correct, all columns and rows will add to the same number.

A. BENEVOLENCE
B. ANNIHILATE
C. CENSURED
D. INCOHERENT
E. EMANCIPATION
F. VIGILANCE

G. AUTHENTIC
H. MAXIM
I. IMBUE
J. ABHORRENCE
K. DEFICIENCY
L. DEPRAVITY

M. SCANTY
N. ODIOUSNESS
O. DESTITUTE
P. MANIFESTATION

1. Totally lacking
2. Intense disapproval or dislike
3. Saying; a truth
4. Kindness; compassion; good will
5. Rambling; confused; disjointed
6. Setting free
7. Lack; shortage
8. Being full of hatred
9. Care; watchfulness
10. Severely criticized
11. Less than is needed
12. Evil; wickedness
13. Fill
14. Expression; revelation; display
15. Destroy
16. Genuine; real

| A= | B= | C= | D= |
| E= | F= | G= | H= |
| I= | J= | K= | L= |
| M= | N= | O= | P= |

Frederick Douglass Vocabulary Magic Squares 1 Answer Key

Match the definition with the vocabulary word. Put your answers in the magic squares below. When your answers are correct, all columns and rows will add to the same number.

A. BENEVOLENCE
B. ANNIHILATE
C. CENSURED
D. INCOHERENT
E. EMANCIPATION
F. VIGILANCE
G. AUTHENTIC
H. MAXIM
I. IMBUE
J. ABHORRENCE
K. DEFICIENCY
L. DEPRAVITY
M. SCANTY
N. ODIOUSNESS
O. DESTITUTE
P. MANIFESTATION

1. Totally lacking
2. Intense disapproval or dislike
3. Saying; a truth
4. Kindness; compassion; good will
5. Rambling; confused; disjointed
6. Setting free
7. Lack; shortage
8. Being full of hatred
9. Care; watchfulness
10. Severely criticized
11. Less than is needed
12. Evil; wickedness
13. Fill
14. Expression; revelation; display
15. Destroy
16. Genuine; real

| A=4 | B=15 | C=10 | D=5 |
| E=6 | F=9 | G=16 | H=3 |
| I=13 | J=2 | K=7 | L=12 |
| M=11 | N=8 | O=1 | P=14 |

Frederick Douglass Vocabulary Magic Squares 2

Match the definition with the vocabulary word. Put your answers in the magic squares below. When your answers are correct, all columns and rows will add to the same number.

A. INFIDEL
B. AGITATED
C. PROVIDENCE
D. SCANTY
E. AVAILED
F. APPALLED
G. VINDICATION
H. SAGACITY
I. SCATHING
J. IMMUTABLE
K. AUTHENTIC
L. RAPTURE
M. COMMENSURATE
N. IMBUE
O. DESTITUTE
P. ABHORRENCE

1. A person without belief in the religion of the writer
2. Fill
3. Not changeable
4. Made useful; helped
5. Support; justification
6. Delight; joy
7. Intense disapproval or dislike
8. Care or guardianship exercised by a deity
9. Totally lacking
10. Less than is needed
11. Wisdom
12. Genuine; real
13. Scornful; mocking
14. Shocked; horrified
15. Anxious; nervous
16. Equal

| A= | B= | C= | D= |
| E= | F= | G= | H= |
| I= | J= | K= | L= |
| M= | N= | O= | P= |

Frederick Douglass Vocabulary Magic Squares 2 Answer Key

Match the definition with the vocabulary word. Put your answers in the magic squares below. When your answers are correct, all columns and rows will add to the same number.

A. INFIDEL
B. AGITATED
C. PROVIDENCE
D. SCANTY
E. AVAILED
F. APPALLED
G. VINDICATION
H. SAGACITY
I. SCATHING
J. IMMUTABLE
K. AUTHENTIC
L. RAPTURE
M. COMMENSURATE
N. IMBUE
O. DESTITUTE
P. ABHORRENCE

1. A person without belief in the religion of the writer
2. Fill
3. Not changeable
4. Made useful; helped
5. Support; justification
6. Delight; joy
7. Intense disapproval or dislike
8. Care or guardianship exercised by a deity
9. Totally lacking
10. Less than is needed
11. Wisdom
12. Genuine; real
13. Scornful; mocking
14. Shocked; horrified
15. Anxious; nervous
16. Equal

| A=1 | B=15 | C=8 | D=10 |
| --- | --- | --- | --- |
| E=4 | F=14 | G=5 | H=11 |
| I=13 | J=3 | K=12 | L=6 |
| M=16 | N=2 | O=9 | P=7 |

Frederick Douglass Vocabulary Magic Squares 3

Match the definition with the vocabulary word. Put your answers in the magic squares below. When your answers are correct, all columns and rows will add to the same number.

A. CONJECTURE
B. IMMUTABLE
C. SAGACITY
D. SCATHING
E. PROFLIGATE
F. DESTITUTE
G. MANIFESTATION
H. VINDICATION
I. OBDURATE
J. ARDENTLY
K. VIGILANCE
L. DESOLATE
M. SUNDERED
N. ABHORRENCE
O. DENUNCIATION
P. EXCULPATE

1. Separated
2. Totally lacking
3. Support; justification
4. Condemnation; criticism
5. Deserted; uninhabited
6. Wisdom
7. Guessing
8. Enthusiastically
9. Care; watchfulness
10. Scornful; mocking
11. Not changeable
12. Stubborn
13. Intense disapproval or dislike
14. Wasteful; extremely extravagant
15. Expression; revelation; display
16. To free from blame

| A= | B= | C= | D= |
|---|---|---|---|
| E= | F= | G= | H= |
| I= | J= | K= | L= |
| M= | N= | O= | P= |

82
Copyrighted

Frederick Douglass Vocabulary Magic Squares 3 Answer Key

Match the definition with the vocabulary word. Put your answers in the magic squares below. When your answers are correct, all columns and rows will add to the same number.

A. CONJECTURE
B. IMMUTABLE
C. SAGACITY
D. SCATHING
E. PROFLIGATE
F. DESTITUTE
G. MANIFESTATION
H. VINDICATION
I. OBDURATE
J. ARDENTLY
K. VIGILANCE
L. DESOLATE
M. SUNDERED
N. ABHORRENCE
O. DENUNCIATION
P. EXCULPATE

1. Separated
2. Totally lacking
3. Support; justification
4. Condemnation; criticism
5. Deserted; uninhabited
6. Wisdom
7. Guessing
8. Enthusiastically
9. Care; watchfulness
10. Scornful; mocking
11. Not changeable
12. Stubborn
13. Intense disapproval or dislike
14. Wasteful; extremely extravagant
15. Expression; revelation; display
16. To free from blame

| A=7 | B=11 | C=6 | D=10 |
| --- | --- | --- | --- |
| E=14 | F=2 | G=15 | H=3 |
| I=12 | J=8 | K=9 | L=5 |
| M=1 | N=13 | O=4 | P=16 |

Frederick Douglass Vocabulary Magic Squares 4

Match the definition with the vocabulary word. Put your answers in the magic squares below. When your answers are correct, all columns and rows will add to the same number.

A. PROFLIGATE
B. QUAILED
C. IMBIBED
D. ANNIHILATE
E. AUTHENTIC
F. PERDITION
G. CENSURED
H. AGITATED
I. BENEVOLENCE
J. SCATHING
K. IMBUE
L. DEFILED
M. SUNDERED
N. OBDURATE
O. RETALIATION
P. DESTITUTE

1. Anxious; nervous
2. Wasteful; extremely extravagant
3. Drew back in fear
4. Severely criticized
5. Scornful; mocking
6. Revenge; getting even
7. Totally lacking
8. Kindness; compassion; good will
9. Fill
10. Stubborn
11. Separated
12. Having one's good name ruined
13. Genuine; real
14. Destroy
15. Took into the mind; absorbed
16. State of everlasting punishment; hell

| A= | B= | C= | D= |
|---|---|---|---|
| E= | F= | G= | H= |
| I= | J= | K= | L= |
| M= | N= | O= | P= |

Frederick Douglass Vocabulary Magic Squares 4 Answer Key

Match the definition with the vocabulary word. Put your answers in the magic squares below. When your answers are correct, all columns and rows will add to the same number.

A. PROFLIGATE
B. QUAILED
C. IMBIBED
D. ANNIHILATE
E. AUTHENTIC
F. PERDITION
G. CENSURED
H. AGITATED
I. BENEVOLENCE
J. SCATHING
K. IMBUE
L. DEFILED
M. SUNDERED
N. OBDURATE
O. RETALIATION
P. DESTITUTE

1. Anxious; nervous
2. Wasteful; extremely extravagant
3. Drew back in fear
4. Severely criticized
5. Scornful; mocking
6. Revenge; getting even
7. Totally lacking
8. Kindness; compassion; good will
9. Fill
10. Stubborn
11. Separated
12. Having one's good name ruined
13. Genuine; real
14. Destroy
15. Took into the mind; absorbed
16. State of everlasting punishment; hell

| A=2 | B=3 | C=15 | D=14 |
|---|---|---|---|
| E=13 | F=16 | G=4 | H=1 |
| I=8 | J=5 | K=9 | L=12 |
| M=11 | N=10 | O=6 | P=7 |

# Frederick Douglass Vocabulary Word Search 1

```
E D K E I Q R C A B I M P U T A T I O N S
T P E C M R U B N S N P B V S Q X V R T B
A R S N P K Z A N Q F S Q K D R Y A S N E
M O C E U B M I I T I E X C U L P A T E N
M V A R D N Q N H L D W C Y T T G V T R E
U I N R E D C O I H E C L N U A L A I E V
S D T O N E Y I L Y L D E R C A R I M H O
N E Y H C P T T A M Z D E I P U O L B O L
O N T B E R M A T T R W T Q S T D E I C E
C C Y A W A A T E A I Y V N D H I D B N N
I E D V X V G S E D V O E P A E O M E I C
M M N I T I I E R E E M N R I N U A D M E
P A M S D T T T U S M F L O R T S N V M D
E N H B U Y A E T O A H I F Y I N I I U E
R C F P R R T D C L P F S L M C E F G T F
T I P D E S E Y E A P C C I E R S E I A I
I P E E T U D D J T A B A G P D S S L B C
N A R S A N Y K N E L Y T A W S M T A L I
E T P T L D H G O Z L P H T R R M A N E E
N I L I I E Q F C C E P I E V N H T C L N
T O E T A R W Y R H D L N N C W L I E G C
D N X U T E Z D B L S B G D H Z H O M R Y
N O I T I D R E P H W S U O I C I N R E P
T V N E O R Z V V I N D I C A T I O N P Q
J N G D N O B D U R A T E X H O R T E D F
```

A person without belief in the religion of the writer (7)
Accusations (11)
Anxious; nervous (8)
Being full of hatred (10)
Care or guardianship exercised by a deity (10)
Care; watchfulness (9)
Complete (10)
Condemnation; criticism (12)
Delight; joy (7)
Deserted; uninhabited (8)
Destroy (10)
Destructive; harmful (10)
Drew back in fear (7)
Enthusiastically (8)
Equal (12)
Evil; wickedness (9)
Expression; revelation; display (13)
Fill (5)
Genuine; real (9)
Guessing (10)
Hatred; loathing (11)
Having one's good name ruined (7)
Huge numbers (7)
Intense disapproval or dislike (10)

Kindness; compassion; good will (11)
Lack; shortage (10)
Less than is needed (6)
Made useful; helped (7)
Not changeable (9)
Puzzling; confusing (10)
Rambling; confused; disjointed (10)
Revenge; getting even (11)
Rude behavior (9)
Rude; disrespectful (11)
Saying; a truth (5)
Scornful; mocking (8)
Separated (8)
Setting free (12)
Severely criticized (8)
Shocked; horrified (8)
State of everlasting punishment; hell (9)
Stubborn (8)
Support; justification (11)
To free from blame (9)
Took into the mind; absorbed (7)
Totally lacking (9)
Urged; insisted (8)
Wasteful; extremely extravagant (10)
Wisdom (8)

# Frederick Douglass Vocabulary Word Search 1 Answer Key

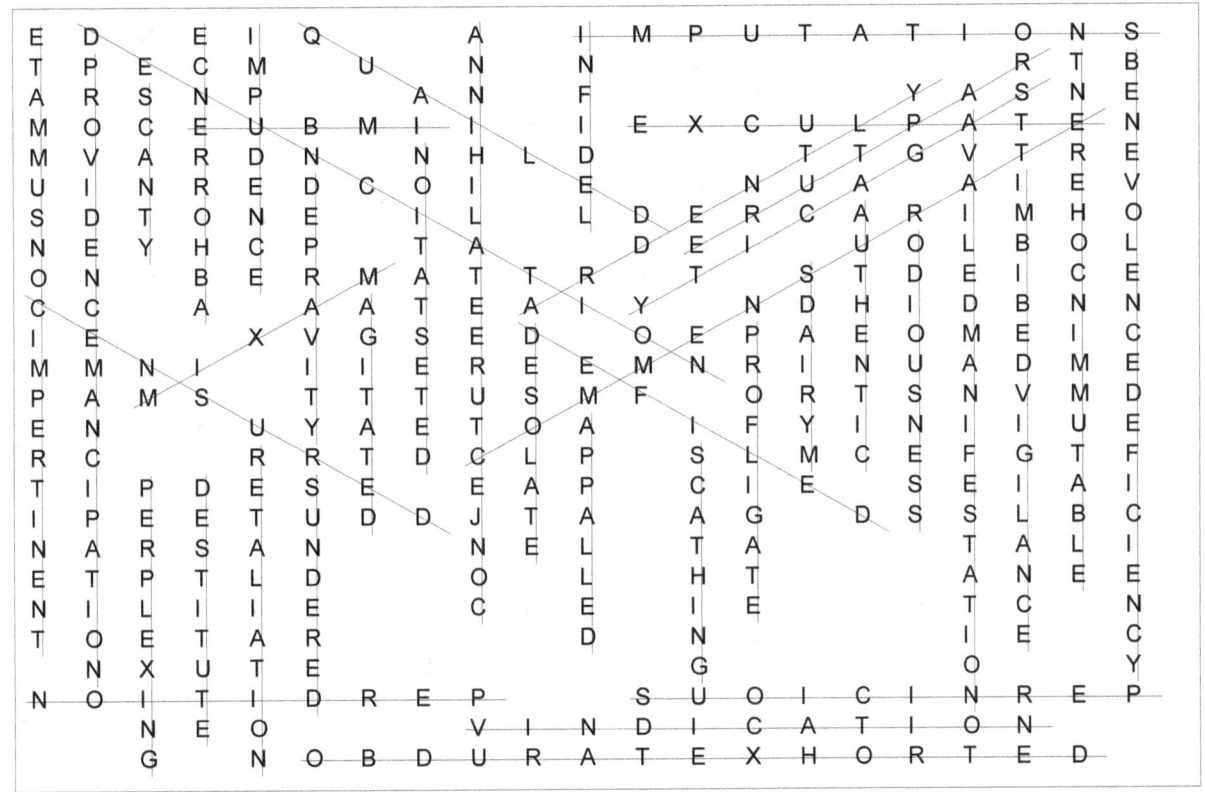

A person without belief in the religion of the writer (7)
Accusations (11)
Anxious; nervous (8)
Being full of hatred (10)
Care or guardianship exercised by a deity (10)
Care; watchfulness (9)
Complete (10)
Condemnation; criticism (12)
Delight; joy (7)
Deserted; uninhabited (8)
Destroy (10)
Destructive; harmful (10)
Drew back in fear (7)
Enthusiastically (8)
Equal (12)
Evil; wickedness (9)
Expression; revelation; display (13)
Fill (5)
Genuine; real (9)
Guessing (10)
Hatred; loathing (11)
Having one's good name ruined (7)
Huge numbers (7)
Intense disapproval or dislike (10)

Kindness; compassion; good will (11)
Lack; shortage (10)
Less than is needed (6)
Made useful; helped (7)
Not changeable (9)
Puzzling; confusing (10)
Rambling; confused; disjointed (10)
Revenge; getting even (11)
Rude behavior (9)
Rude; disrespectful (11)
Saying; a truth (5)
Scornful; mocking (8)
Separated (8)
Setting free (12)
Severely criticized (8)
Shocked; horrified (8)
State of everlasting punishment; hell (9)
Stubborn (8)
Support; justification (11)
To free from blame (9)
Took into the mind; absorbed (7)
Totally lacking (9)
Urged; insisted (8)
Wasteful; extremely extravagant (10)
Wisdom (8)

# Frederick Douglass Vocabulary Word Search 2

```
O F N A I M P U D E N C E S C A T H I N G
A D O E U F G C T V J Z C X D R D Q W X N
B T I H X T R C M W R D C N V H C C N Y H I
H N T O Q C H E R U T C E J N O C O B M X
O E A P U Z U E K N T D A V M R I E G E
R R C E M S T L N F M Q I P I M Q T N Y L
R E I R A A N S P T C X V P G E U A E W P
E H D N N V E E A A I P O A I N A P V D R
N O N I I A N L S G T C R L S I I O C E
C C I C F I I B O S A E P L A U L C L O P
E N V I E L T A B A M C W E N R E N E N Q
R I D O S E R T D B G J I D C A D A N S B
E M H U T D E U U J P I Z T E T E M C U N
T P D S A L P M R L R K T M Y E F E E M O
A U E Q T V M M A F O X M A D L I F V M I
L T P J I X I I T H F X A E T Q L V A A T
I A R Y O D Z F E V L R N T C E E R Y T I
A T A W N N O I T A I C N U N E D T S E D
T I V I L G M M M L G H I T D E N X U E R
I O I Q M P A D E V A V H I N A J B R R E
O N T J Q B X D Z N T C I T C D M E L U P
N S Y C N E I C I F E D L S S I D F W T F
M D C N X F M B S R T Y A E J N P W G P Z
M R C E N S U R E D J X T D U T M N K A N
M Y R I A D S P X D R D E S O L A T E R Q
```

A person without belief in the religion of the writer (7)
Accusations (11)
Anxious; nervous (8)
Being full of hatred (10)
Care or guardianship exercised by a deity (10)
Care; watchfulness (9)
Complete (10)
Condemnation; criticism (12)
Delight; joy (7)
Deserted; uninhabited (8)
Destroy (10)
Destructive; harmful (10)
Drew back in fear (7)
Enthusiastically (8)
Equal (12)
Evil; wickedness (9)
Expression; revelation; display (13)
Fill (5)
Genuine; real (9)
Guessing (10)
Having one's good name ruined (7)
Huge numbers (7)
Intense disapproval or dislike (10)
Kindness; compassion; good will (11)

Lack; shortage (10)
Less than is needed (6)
Made useful; helped (7)
Not changeable (9)
Puzzling; confusing (10)
Rambling; confused; disjointed (10)
Revenge; getting even (11)
Rude behavior (9)
Rude; disrespectful (11)
Saying; a truth (5)
Scornful; mocking (8)
Separated (8)
Setting free (12)
Severely criticized (8)
Shocked; horrified (8)
State of everlasting punishment; hell (9)
Stubborn (8)
Support; justification (11)
To free from blame (9)
Took into the mind; absorbed (7)
Totally lacking (9)
Urged; insisted (8)
Wasteful; extremely extravagant (10)
Wisdom (8)

# Frederick Douglass Vocabulary Word Search 2 Answer Key

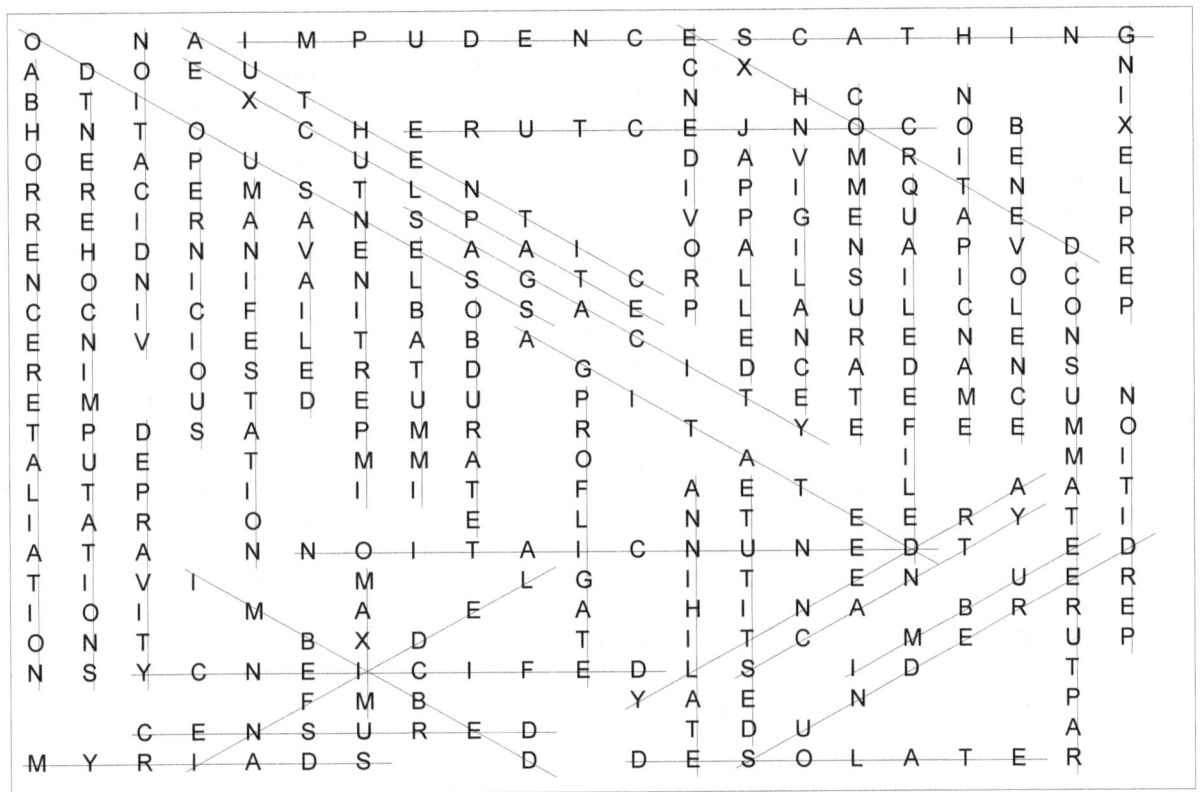

A person without belief in the religion of the writer (7)
Accusations (11)
Anxious; nervous (8)
Being full of hatred (10)
Care or guardianship exercised by a deity (10)
Care; watchfulness (9)
Complete (10)
Condemnation; criticism (12)
Delight; joy (7)
Deserted; uninhabited (8)
Destroy (10)
Destructive; harmful (10)
Drew back in fear (7)
Enthusiastically (8)
Equal (12)
Evil; wickedness (9)
Expression; revelation; display (13)
Fill (5)
Genuine; real (9)
Guessing (10)
Having one's good name ruined (7)
Huge numbers (7)
Intense disapproval or dislike (10)
Kindness; compassion; good will (11)

Lack; shortage (10)
Less than is needed (6)
Made useful; helped (7)
Not changeable (9)
Puzzling; confusing (10)
Rambling; confused; disjointed (10)
Revenge; getting even (11)
Rude behavior (9)
Rude; disrespectful (11)
Saying; a truth (5)
Scornful; mocking (8)
Separated (8)
Setting free (12)
Severely criticized (8)
Shocked; horrified (8)
State of everlasting punishment; hell (9)
Stubborn (8)
Support; justification (11)
To free from blame (9)
Took into the mind; absorbed (7)
Totally lacking (9)
Urged; insisted (8)
Wasteful; extremely extravagant (10)
Wisdom (8)

# Frederick Douglass Vocabulary Word Search 3

```
S A G A C I T Y J B J J D B S I L B M Q
F Q H Y V H C F V T V S N O S U M M J D Q
K U G T I L F W L B A C V M B N K N B K B
W A G N J M Q C A G I T A T E D P X E U E
R I M A T P P C R V L L B C E E U C C F N
D L D C V K L E Y C E Y N F L R N R N Q E
C E N S U R E D R G D E I E Y E E E A T V
I D P T Y L G L G T D C D L R D T C L T O
R M N R J W H D U I I T R B A U N I A L
E X M S A B N E P E F N O V L C T E G L E
T X X U G V T M N N E H O Y Y O I D I H N
A N C F T R I C I D B R S N M N T I V H C
L S Y U O A Y T R A F E F P T S S V S I E
I S J H L L B A Y S D N W E I U E O M N N
A Z X J R P G L U P O O R M M D R S N O
T E S V M D A O E I P I D P Y M B P K A T
I M A X I M I T T P R T I L R A G I L W A
O D Z S W C F A E E O A O E I T N A B R C
N L V S I D I D W R F P U X A E I P A E I
W W B N X C L E H D L I S I D C H P C Z D
K V R G N S N F T I I C N N S G T A B S N
S E M U K Z J I Y T G N E G R U A L D G I
P D N D Y Q M L G I A A S P R R C L N L V
N E Q Z W B M E V O T M S E K V S E H C X
D P P L F B S D K N E E X V P J D D C S C
```

ABHORRENCE

AGITATED

ANNIHILATE

APPALLED

ARDENTLY

AVAILED

BENEVOLENCE

CENSURED

CONSUMMATE

DEFICIENCY

DEFILED

DENUNCIATION

DEPRAVITY

DESOLATE

DESTITUTE

EMANCIPATION

EXCULPATE

EXHORTED

IMBIBED

IMBUE

IMMUTABLE

IMPERTINENT

IMPUDENCE

INFIDEL

MAXIM

MYRIADS

OBDURATE

ODIOUSNESS

PERDITION

PERNICIOUS

PERPLEXING

PROFLIGATE

PROVIDENCE

QUAILED

RAPTURE

RETALIATION

SAGACITY

SCANTY

SCATHING

SUNDERED

VIGILANCE

VINDICATION

# Frederick Douglass Vocabulary Word Search 3 Answer Key

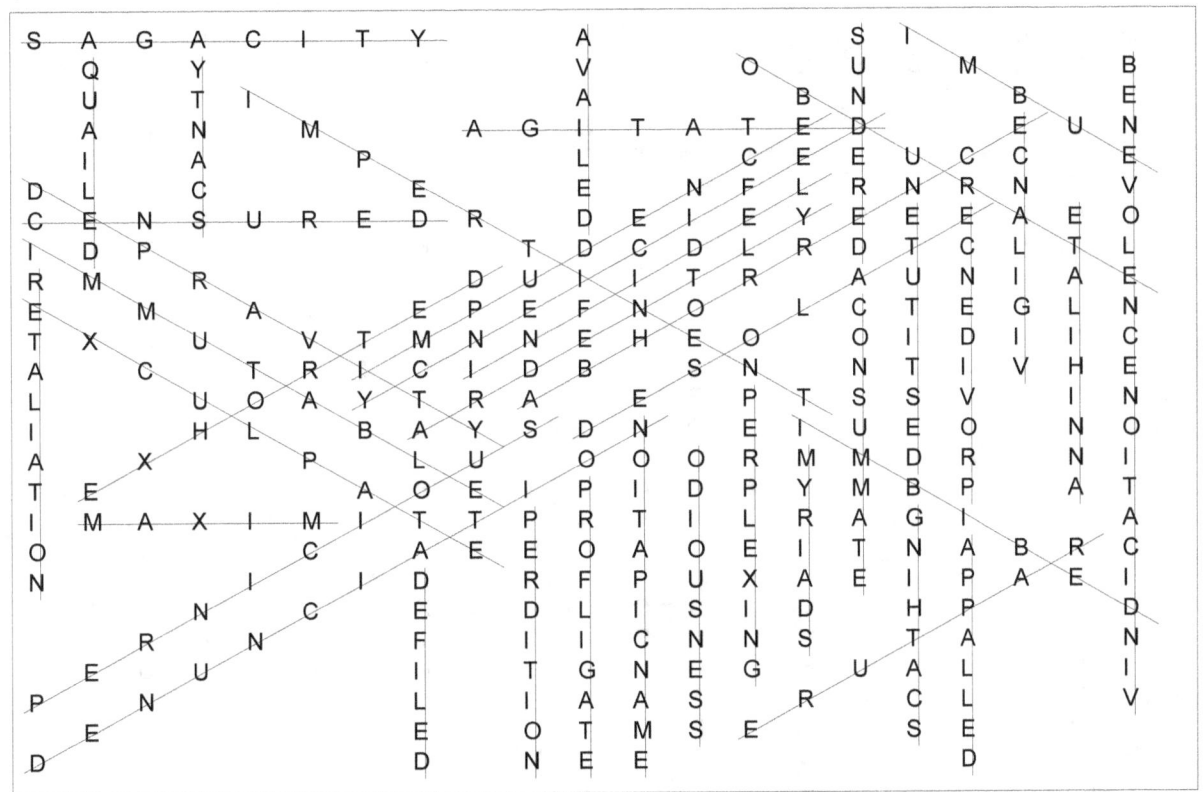

| ABHORRENCE | DESTITUTE | PERDITION |
| --- | --- | --- |
| AGITATED | EMANCIPATION | PERNICIOUS |
| ANNIHILATE | EXCULPATE | PERPLEXING |
| APPALLED | EXHORTED | PROFLIGATE |
| ARDENTLY | IMBIBED | PROVIDENCE |
| AVAILED | IMBUE | QUAILED |
| BENEVOLENCE | IMMUTABLE | RAPTURE |
| CENSURED | IMPERTINENT | RETALIATION |
| CONSUMMATE | IMPUDENCE | SAGACITY |
| DEFICIENCY | INFIDEL | SCANTY |
| DEFILED | MAXIM | SCATHING |
| DENUNCIATION | MYRIADS | SUNDERED |
| DEPRAVITY | OBDURATE | VIGILANCE |
| DESOLATE | ODIOUSNESS | VINDICATION |

# Frederick Douglass Vocabulary Word Search 4

```
I  M  B  U  E  A  P  P  A  L  L  E  D  M  M  Z  A  R  G  M  P
S  K  W  N  D  D  D  E  F  I  L  E  D  P  K  G  C  N  N  A  P
V  I  N  D  I  C  A  T  I  O  N  R  L  S  I  K  I  Z  T  N  E
G  E  C  N  A  L  I  G  I  V  A  E  Z  T  G  X  F  H  P  I  R
M  J  G  Y  B  C  N  R  X  P  T  D  A  H  E  K  R  P  S  F  N
A  C  X  C  H  H  H  S  T  A  R  T  C  L  G  K  S  S  F  E  I
I  U  C  Z  O  S  K  U  M  L  E  O  P  L  J  X  E  S  E  S  C
M  H  T  B  R  H  R  M  T  D  L  R  F  R  M  N  W  A  T  T  I
P  B  Y  H  R  E  U  L  Y  S  E  N  G  L  S  T  X  G  A  A  O
E  D  T  S  E  S  D  A  B  P  C  S  S  U  I  L  D  A  R  T  U
R  Q  N  N  N  N  K  V  H  G  N  D  O  S  Z  G  Z  C  U  I  S
T  T  A  O  C  C  T  A  N  K  E  I  N  L  M  Z  A  I  S  O  D
I  Y  C  N  E  I  C  I  F  E  D  E  L  I  A  U  Q  T  N  N  R
N  M  S  O  N  J  H  L  C  O  U  E  X  P  A  T  N  Y  E  A  E
E  S  P  X  N  T  L  E  M  W  P  A  T  N  B  E  E  D  M  R  T
N  U  C  U  A  J  M  D  E  T  M  Q  N  E  R  Q  S  E  M  D  A
T  N  I  C  T  H  E  E  I  X  I  I  P  E  S  S  V  S  O  E  L
S  D  S  M  T  A  T  C  G  N  H  M  H  E  F  T  Z  T  C  N  I
W  E  M  B  B  A  T  K  T  I  F  C  I  M  S  R  V  A  I  G  A
W  R  L  Y  R  T  L  I  L  U  C  I  R  U  X  D  W  T  V  L  T
J  E  Y  U  R  Y  B  A  O  N  R  H  D  T  T  W  I  U  I  Y  I
W  D  D  L  D  I  T  E  I  N  J  E  D  E  E  A  V  T  W  O  O
M  B  K  G  L  E  A  P  D  J  S  Z  X  Z  L  D  B  E  I  K  N
O  G  R  G  V  X  Y  D  E  P  R  A  V  I  T  Y  C  L  S  O  B
C  E  N  S  U  R  E  D  S  P  R  O  V  I  D  E  N  C  E  S  N
```

ABHORRENCE
AGITATED
ANNIHILATE
APPALLED
ARDENTLY
AUTHENTIC
AVAILED
CENSURED
COMMENSURATE
CONJECTURE
CONSUMMATE
DEFICIENCY
DEFILED
DEPRAVITY
DESOLATE

DESTITUTE
DETESTATION
EXHORTED
IMBIBED
IMBUE
IMMUTABLE
IMPERTINENT
IMPUDENCE
IMPUTATIONS
INCOHERENT
INFIDEL
MANIFESTATION
MAXIM
MYRIADS
OBDURATE

ODIOUSNESS
PERDITION
PERNICIOUS
PERPLEXING
PROFLIGATE
PROVIDENCE
QUAILED
RAPTURE
RETALIATION
SAGACITY
SCANTY
SCATHING
SUNDERED
VIGILANCE
VINDICATION

# Frederick Douglass Vocabulary Word Search 4 Answer Key

| ABHORRENCE | DESTITUTE | ODIOUSNESS |
| AGITATED | DETESTATION | PERDITION |
| ANNIHILATE | EXHORTED | PERNICIOUS |
| APPALLED | IMBIBED | PERPLEXING |
| ARDENTLY | IMBUE | PROFLIGATE |
| AUTHENTIC | IMMUTABLE | PROVIDENCE |
| AVAILED | IMPERTINENT | QUAILED |
| CENSURED | IMPUDENCE | RAPTURE |
| COMMENSURATE | IMPUTATIONS | RETALIATION |
| CONJECTURE | INCOHERENT | SAGACITY |
| CONSUMMATE | INFIDEL | SCANTY |
| DEFICIENCY | MANIFESTATION | SCATHING |
| DEFILED | MAXIM | SUNDERED |
| DEPRAVITY | MYRIADS | VIGILANCE |
| DESOLATE | OBDURATE | VINDICATION |

# Frederick Douglass Vocabulary Crossword 1

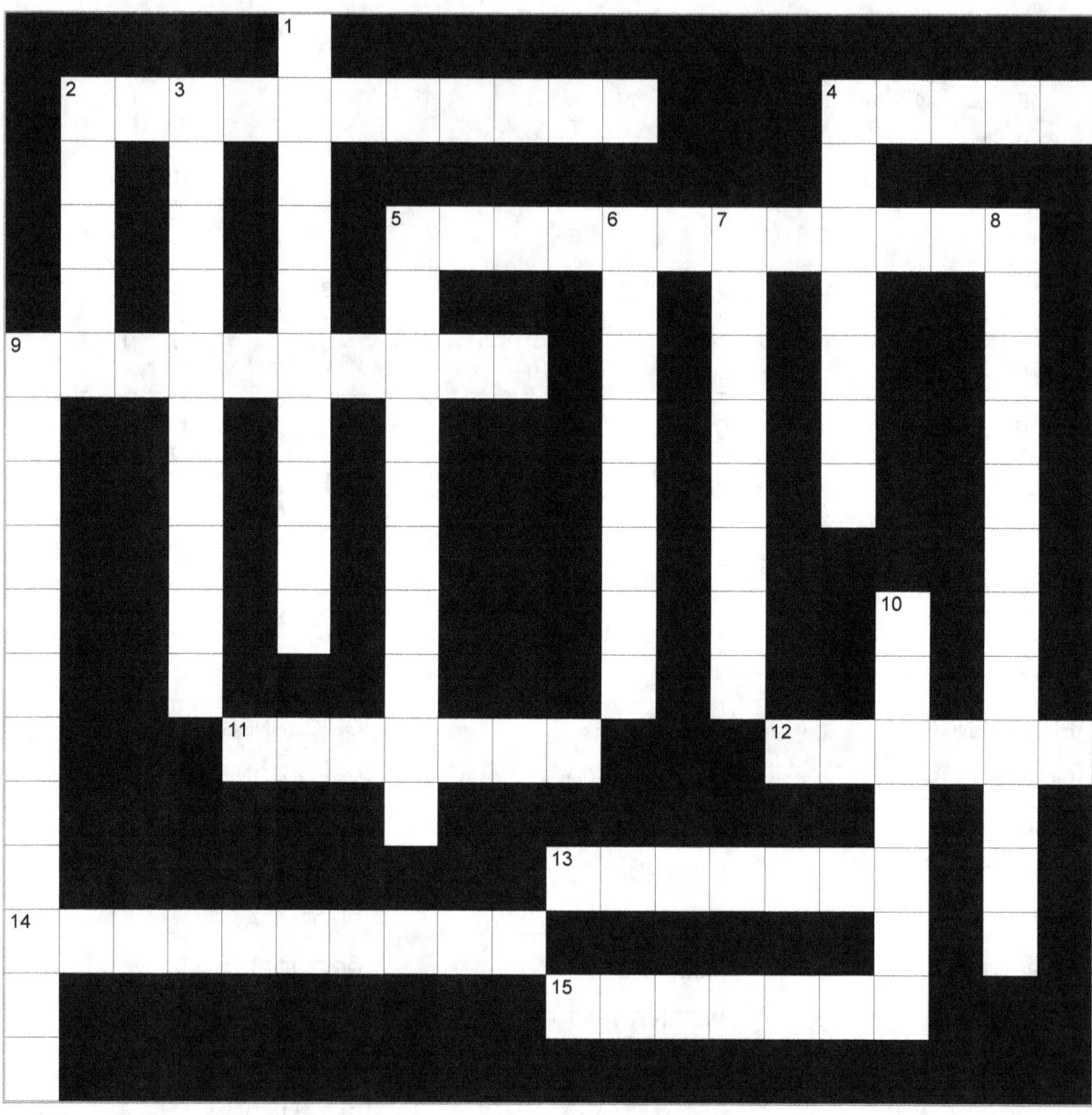

**Across**
2. Rude; disrespectful
4. Saying; a truth
5. Equal
9. Lack; shortage
11. Delight; joy
12. Less than is needed
13. A person without belief in the religion of the writer
14. Rambling; confused; disjointed
15. Took into the mind; absorbed

**Down**
1. Wasteful; extremely extravagant
2. Fill
3. Care or guardianship exercised by a deity
4. Huge numbers
5. Complete
6. Urged; insisted
7. Separated
8. Setting free
9. Condemnation; criticism
10. Made useful; helped

# Frederick Douglass Vocabulary Crossword 1 Answer Key

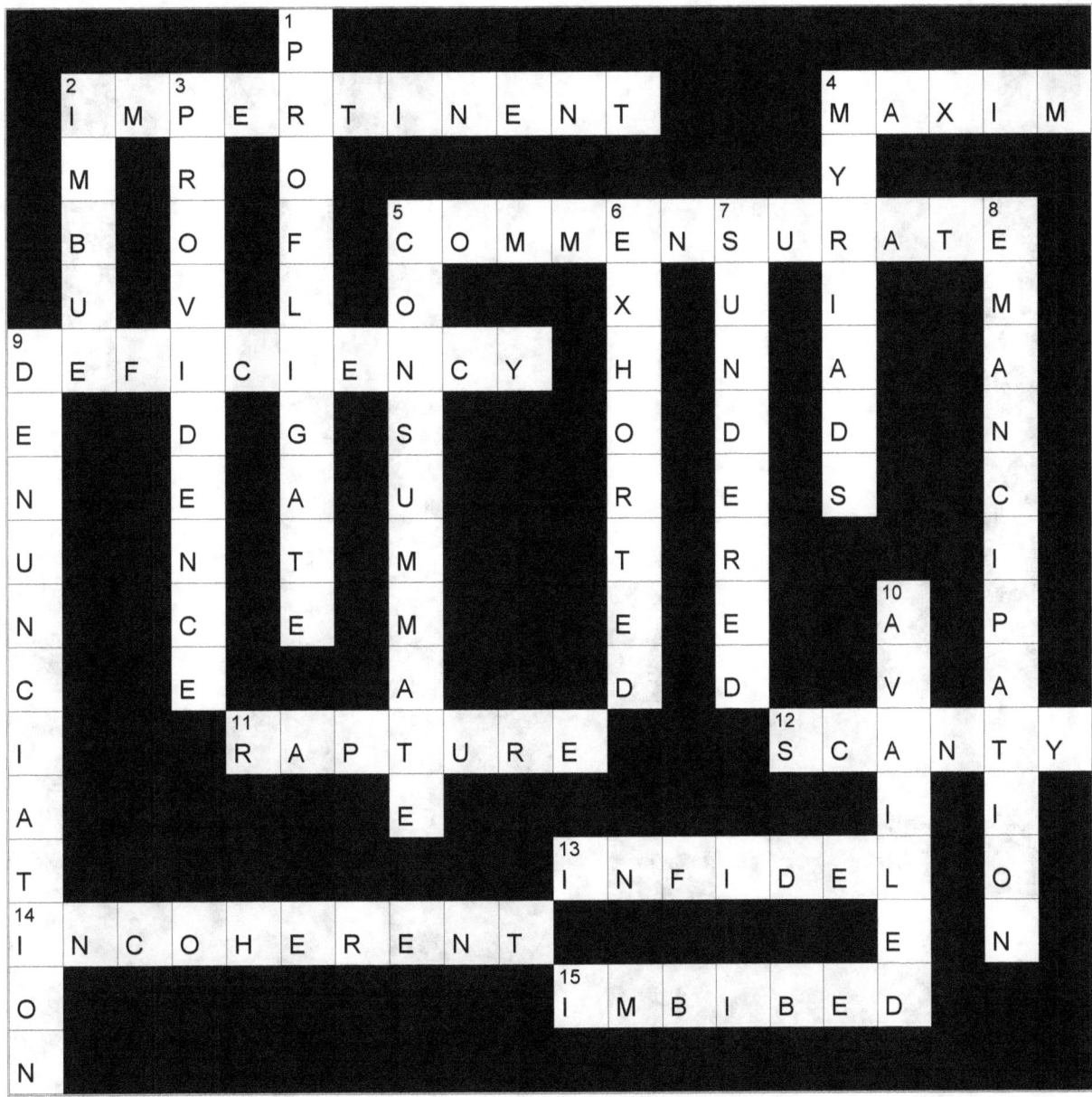

Across
- 2. Rude; disrespectful
- 4. Saying; a truth
- 5. Equal
- 9. Lack; shortage
- 11. Delight; joy
- 12. Less than is needed
- 13. A person without belief in the religion of the writer
- 14. Rambling; confused; disjointed
- 15. Took into the mind; absorbed

Down
- 1. Wasteful; extremely extravagant
- 2. Fill
- 3. Care or guardianship exercised by a deity
- 4. Huge numbers
- 5. Complete
- 6. Urged; insisted
- 7. Separated
- 8. Setting free
- 9. Condemnation; criticism
- 10. Made useful; helped

# Frederick Douglass Vocabulary Crossword 2

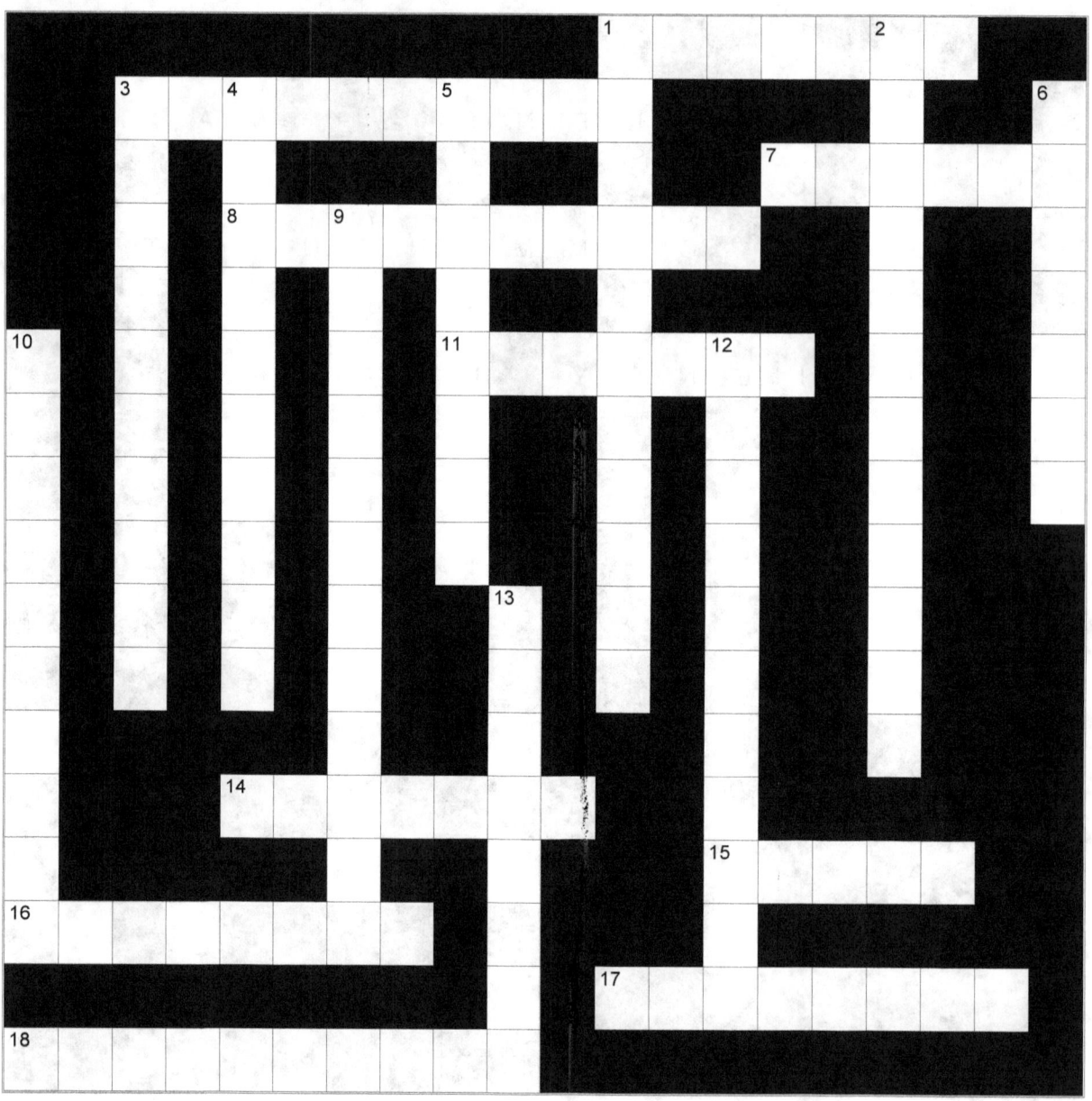

**Across**
1. Having one's good name ruined
3. Care or guardianship exercised by a deity
7. Less than is needed
8. Rambling; confused; disjointed
11. Delight; joy
14. Made useful; helped
15. Fill
16. Separated
17. Severely criticized
18. Lack; shortage

**Down**
1. Hatred; loathing
2. Setting free
3. Wasteful; extremely extravagant
4. Being full of hatred
5. Urged; insisted
6. Huge numbers
9. Equal
10. Destructive; harmful
12. Revenge; getting even
13. Enthusiastically

Frederick Douglass Vocabulary Crossword 2 Answer Key

Across
1. Having one's good name ruined
3. Care or guardianship exercised by a deity
7. Less than is needed
8. Rambling; confused; disjointed
11. Delight; joy
14. Made useful; helped
15. Fill
16. Separated
17. Severely criticized
18. Lack; shortage

Down
1. Hatred; loathing
2. Setting free
3. Wasteful; extremely extravagant
4. Being full of hatred
5. Urged; insisted
6. Huge numbers
9. Equal
10. Destructive; harmful
12. Revenge; getting even
13. Enthusiastically

# Frederick Douglass Vocabulary Crossword 3

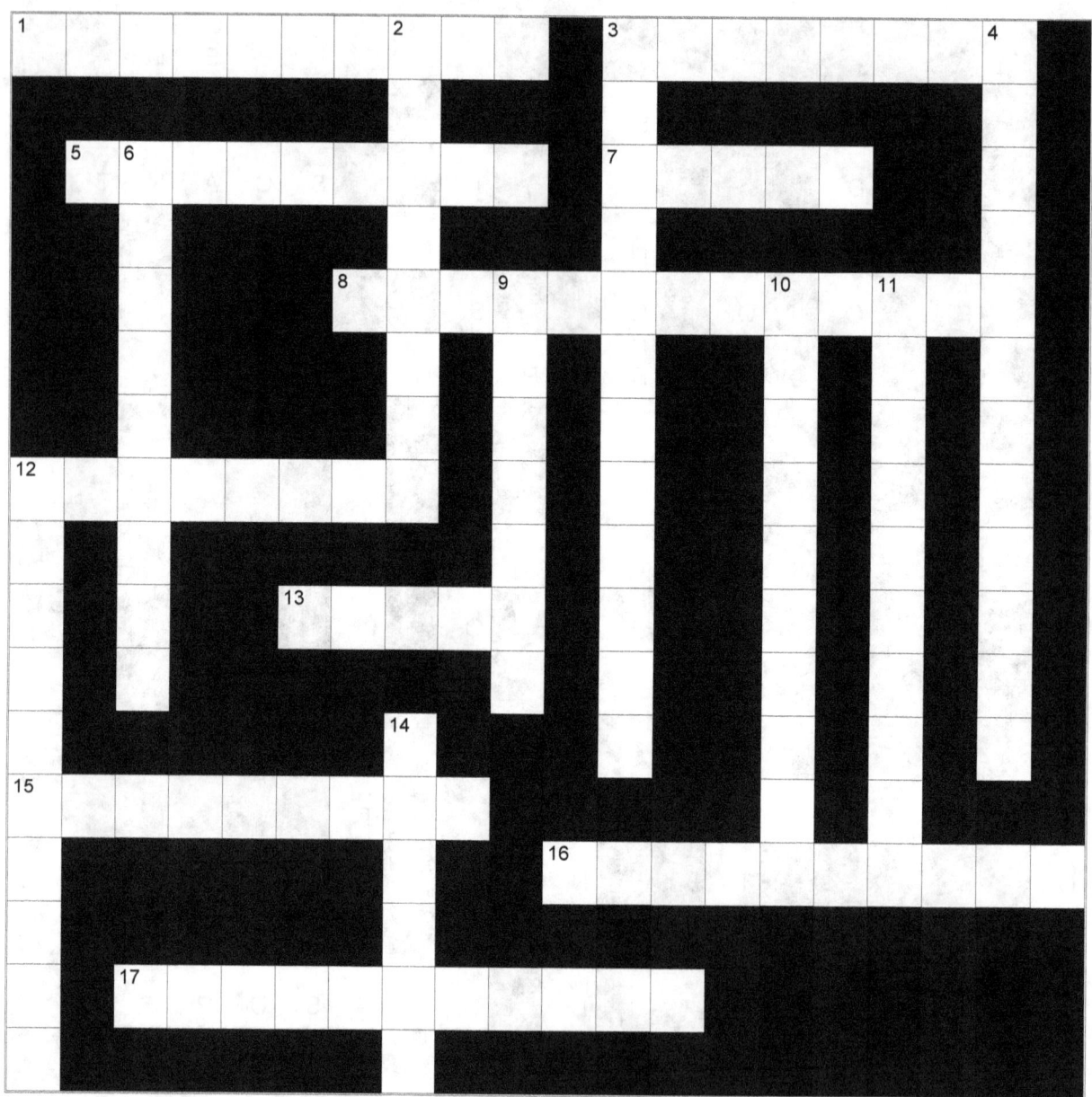

Across
1. Wasteful; extremely extravagant
3. Severely criticized
5. State of everlasting punishment; hell
7. Saying; a truth
8. Expression; revelation; display
12. Shocked; horrified
13. Fill
15. Rude behavior
16. Guessing
17. Rude; disrespectful

Down
2. Anxious; nervous
3. Equal
4. Condemnation; criticism
6. To free from blame
9. A person without belief in the religion of the writer
10. Intense disapproval or dislike
11. Rambling; confused; disjointed
12. Destroy
14. Less than is needed

# Frederick Douglass Vocabulary Crossword 3 Answer Key

**Across**
1. Wasteful; extremely extravagant
3. Severely criticized
5. State of everlasting punishment; hell
7. Saying; a truth
8. Expression; revelation; display
12. Shocked; horrified
13. Fill
15. Rude behavior
16. Guessing
17. Rude; disrespectful

**Down**
2. Anxious; nervous
3. Equal
4. Condemnation; criticism
6. To free from blame
9. A person without belief in the religion of the writer
10. Intense disapproval or dislike
11. Rambling; confused; disjointed
12. Destroy
14. Less than is needed

# Frederick Douglass Vocabulary Crossword 4

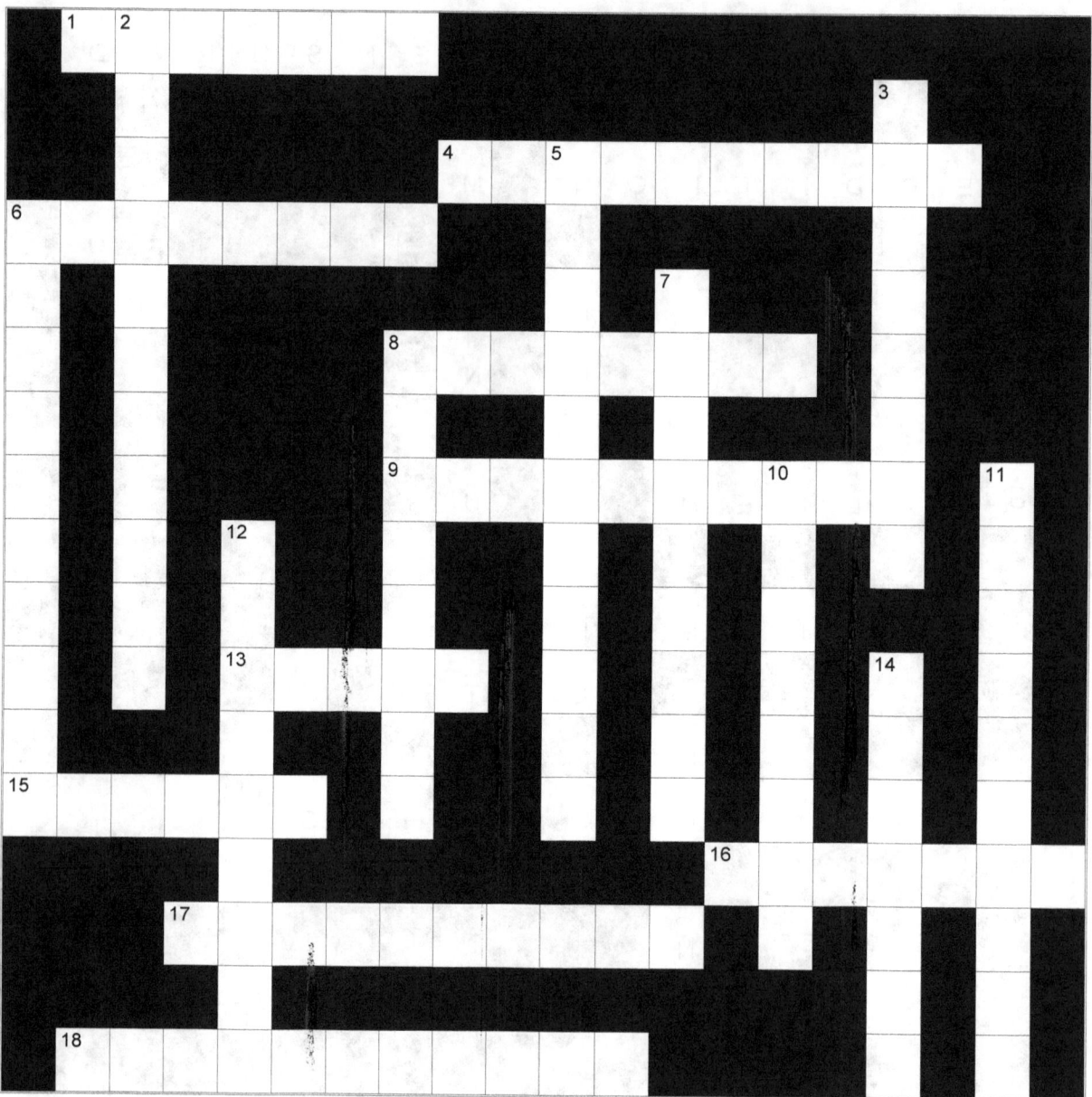

**Across**
1. Made useful; helped
4. Destructive; harmful
6. Stubborn
8. Wisdom
9. Destroy
13. Saying; a truth
15. Less than is needed
16. Having one's good name ruined
17. Intense disapproval or dislike
18. Kindness; compassion; good will

**Down**
2. Support; justification
3. Separated
5. Revenge; getting even
6. Being full of hatred
7. Care; watchfulness
8. Scornful; mocking
10. Shocked; horrified
11. Lack; shortage
12. Not changeable
14. Took into the mind; absorbed

# Frederick Douglass Vocabulary Crossword 4 Answer Key

Across
1. Made useful; helped
4. Destructive; harmful
6. Stubborn
8. Wisdom
9. Destroy
13. Saying; a truth
15. Less than is needed
16. Having one's good name ruined
17. Intense disapproval or dislike
18. Kindness; compassion; good will

Down
2. Support; justification
3. Separated
5. Revenge; getting even
6. Being full of hatred
7. Care; watchfulness
8. Scornful; mocking
10. Shocked; horrified
11. Lack; shortage
12. Not changeable
14. Took into the mind; absorbed

Frederick Douglass Vocabulary Juggle Letters 1

1. BMDEBII = 1. _____
   Took into the mind; absorbed

2. MUALMEITB = 2. _____
   Not changeable

3. TIMPOSTANIU = 3. _____
   Accusations

4. NITCHGAS = 4. _____
   Scornful; mocking

5. UANCIHETT = 5. _____
   Genuine; real

6. EQUIDLA = 6. _____
   Drew back in fear

7. ECOUIPISRN = 7. _____
   Destructive; harmful

8. TETUEIDST = 8. _____
   Totally lacking

9. TDNERIIOP = 9. _____
   State of everlasting punishment; hell

10. EIDNTTSTAEO =10. _____
    Hatred; loathing

11. NOINSAIFATMTE =11. _____
    Expression; revelation; display

12. LDLAAEPP =12. _____
    Shocked; horrified

13. IVAINECGL =13. _____
    Care; watchfulness

14. TROEDXHE =14. _____
    Urged; insisted

Frederick Douglass Vocabulary Juggle Letters 1 Answer Key

1. BMDEBII = 1. IMBIBED
Took into the mind; absorbed

2. MUALMEITB = 2. IMMUTABLE
Not changeable

3. TIMPOSTANIU = 3. IMPUTATIONS
Accusations

4. NITCHGAS = 4. SCATHING
Scornful; mocking

5. UANCIHETT = 5. AUTHENTIC
Genuine; real

6. EQUIDLA = 6. QUAILED
Drew back in fear

7. ECOUIPISRN = 7. PERNICIOUS
Destructive; harmful

8. TETUEIDST = 8. DESTITUTE
Totally lacking

9. TDNERIIOP = 9. PERDITION
State of everlasting punishment; hell

10. EIDNTTSTAEO =10. DETESTATION
Hatred; loathing

11. NOINSAIFATMTE =11. MANIFESTATION
Expression; revelation; display

12. LDLAAEPP =12. APPALLED
Shocked; horrified

13. IVAINECGL =13. VIGILANCE
Care; watchfulness

14. TROEDXHE =14. EXHORTED
Urged; insisted

Frederick Douglass Vocabulary Juggle Letters 2

1. MMTROSUEENCA = 1. _____
   Equal

2. YCASNT = 2. _____
   Less than is needed

3. EAICLVNIG = 3. _____
   Care; watchfulness

4. TIACSNHG = 4. _____
   Scornful; mocking

5. LAADPELP = 5. _____
   Shocked; horrified

6. DPRNIOTIE = 6. _____
   State of everlasting punishment; hell

7. IEPATOAMNCIN = 7. _____
   Setting free

8. OERTCNNIHE = 8. _____
   Rambling; confused; disjointed

9. UCITHETNA = 9. _____
   Genuine; real

10. INVCEOREDP =10. _____
    Care or guardianship exercised by a deity

11. IMUONPTSATI =11. _____
    Accusations

12. OBRCNAERHE =12. _____
    Intense disapproval or dislike

13. ONSODESISU =13. _____
    Being full of hatred

14. SEATMMCUNO =14. _____
    Complete

Frederick Douglass Vocabulary Juggle Letters 2 Answer Key

1. MMTROSUEENCA = 1. COMMENSURATE
Equal

2. YCASNT = 2. SCANTY
Less than is needed

3. EAICLVNIG = 3. VIGILANCE
Care; watchfulness

4. TIACSNHG = 4. SCATHING
Scornful; mocking

5. LAADPELP = 5. APPALLED
Shocked; horrified

6. DPRNIOTIE = 6. PERDITION
State of everlasting punishment; hell

7. IEPATOAMNCIN = 7. EMANCIPATION
Setting free

8. OERTCNNIHE = 8. INCOHERENT
Rambling; confused; disjointed

9. UCITHETNA = 9. AUTHENTIC
Genuine; real

10. INVCEOREDP =10. PROVIDENCE
Care or guardianship exercised by a deity

11. IMUONPTSATI =11. IMPUTATIONS
Accusations

12. OBRCNAERHE =12. ABHORRENCE
Intense disapproval or dislike

13. ONSODESISU =13. ODIOUSNESS
Being full of hatred

14. SEATMMCUNO =14. CONSUMMATE
Complete

Frederick Douglass Vocabulary Juggle Letters 3

1. APLDAEPL = 1. _____
    Shocked; horrified

2. EDEDLFI = 2. _____
    Having one's good name ruined

3. EMIBU = 3. _____
    Fill

4. SNUOECIPRI = 4. _____
    Destructive; harmful

5. IEICFECYND = 5. _____
    Lack; shortage

6. UEATNHTIC = 6. _____
    Genuine; real

7. DESEURND = 7. _____
    Separated

8. OSEAEDTL = 8. _____
    Deserted; uninhabited

9. HROECAENRB = 9. _____
    Intense disapproval or dislike

10. XTHEEORD = 10. _____
    Urged; insisted

11. CNSTYA = 11. _____
    Less than is needed

12. ENOPTIDIR = 12. _____
    State of everlasting punishment; hell

13. LEAINATINH = 13. _____
    Destroy

14. TUECAPELX = 14. _____
    To free from blame

Frederick Douglass Vocabulary Juggle Letters 3 Answer Key

1. APLDAEPL = 1. APPALLED
Shocked; horrified

2. EDEDLFI = 2. DEFILED
Having one's good name ruined

3. EMIBU = 3. IMBUE
Fill

4. SNUOECIPRI = 4. PERNICIOUS
Destructive; harmful

5. IEICFECYND = 5. DEFICIENCY
Lack; shortage

6. UEATNHTIC = 6. AUTHENTIC
Genuine; real

7. DESEURND = 7. SUNDERED
Separated

8. OSEAEDTL = 8. DESOLATE
Deserted; uninhabited

9. HROECAENRB = 9. ABHORRENCE
Intense disapproval or dislike

10. XTHEEORD =10. EXHORTED
Urged; insisted

11. CNSTYA =11. SCANTY
Less than is needed

12. ENOPTIDIR =12. PERDITION
State of everlasting punishment; hell

13. LEAINATINH =13. ANNIHILATE
Destroy

14. TUECAPELX =14. EXCULPATE
To free from blame

Frederick Douglass Vocabulary Juggle Letters 4

1. OREJNCCUTE = 1. _____
   Guessing

2. UIPECDNEM = 2. _____
   Rude behavior

3. ELXNGIPPRE = 3. _____
   Puzzling; confusing

4. BADRUOET = 4. _____
   Stubborn

5. TIUMTASINOP = 5. _____
   Accusations

6. ENBCONELEEV = 6. _____
   Kindness; compassion; good will

7. NEOTNCNIDAUI = 7. _____
   Condemnation; criticism

8. LIOTETIRNAA = 8. _____
   Revenge; getting even

9. IHTCGSAN = 9. _____
   Scornful; mocking

10. BRHENCEOAR =10. _____
    Intense disapproval or dislike

11. INDIAVIONCT =11. _____
    Support; justification

12. EBBMIID =12. _____
    Took into the mind; absorbed

13. MESCOMNATU =13. _____
    Complete

14. URAPRET =14. _____
    Delight; joy

Frederick Douglass Vocabulary Juggle Letters 4 Answer Key

1. OREJNCCUTE = 1. CONJECTURE
Guessing

2. UIPECDNEM = 2. IMPUDENCE
Rude behavior

3. ELXNGIPPRE = 3. PERPLEXING
Puzzling; confusing

4. BADRUOET = 4. OBDURATE
Stubborn

5. TIUMTASINOP = 5. IMPUTATIONS
Accusations

6. ENBCONELEEV = 6. BENEVOLENCE
Kindness; compassion; good will

7. NEOTNCNIDAUI = 7. DENUNCIATION
Condemnation; criticism

8. LIOTETIRNAA = 8. RETALIATION
Revenge; getting even

9. IHTCGSAN = 9. SCATHING
Scornful; mocking

10. BRHENCEOAR =10. ABHORRENCE
Intense disapproval or dislike

11. INDIAVIONCT =11. VINDICATION
Support; justification

12. EBBMIID =12. IMBIBED
Took into the mind; absorbed

13. MESCOMNATU =13. CONSUMMATE
Complete

14. URAPRET =14. RAPTURE
Delight; joy

| | |
|---|---|
| ABHORRENCE | Intense disapproval or dislike |
| AGITATED | Anxious; nervous |
| ANNIHILATE | Destroy |
| APPALLED | Shocked; horrified |
| ARDENTLY | Enthusiastically |

| AUTHENTIC | Genuine; real |
|---|---|
| AVAILED | Made useful; helped |
| BENEVOLENCE | Kindness; compassion; good will |
| CENSURED | Severely criticized |
| COMMENSURATE | Equal |

| CONJECTURE | Guessing |
| --- | --- |
| CONSUMMATE | Complete |
| DEFICIENCY | Lack; shortage |
| DEFILED | Having one's good name ruined |
| DENUNCIATION | Condemnation; criticism |

| | |
|---|---|
| DEPRAVITY | Evil; wickedness |
| DESOLATE | Deserted; uninhabited |
| DESTITUTE | Totally lacking |
| DETESTATION | Hatred; loathing |
| EMANCIPATION | Setting free |

| EXCULPATE | To free from blame |
|---|---|
| EXHORTED | Urged; insisted |
| IMBIBED | Took into the mind; absorbed |
| IMBUE | Fill |
| IMMUTABLE | Not changeable |

| | |
|---|---|
| IMPERTINENT | Rude; disrespectful |
| IMPUDENCE | Rude behavior |
| IMPUTATIONS | Accusations |
| INCOHERENT | Rambling; confused; disjointed |
| INFIDEL | A person without belief in the religion of the writer |

| | |
|---|---|
| MANIFESTATION | Expression; revelation; display |
| MAXIM | Saying; a truth |
| MYRIADS | Huge numbers |
| OBDURATE | Stubborn |
| ODIOUSNESS | Being full of hatred |

| | |
|---|---|
| PERDITION | State of everlasting punishment; hell |
| PERNICIOUS | Destructive; harmful |
| PERPLEXING | Puzzling; confusing |
| PROFLIGATE | Wasteful; extremely extravagant |
| PROVIDENCE | Care or guardianship exercised by a deity |

| | |
|---|---|
| QUAILED | Drew back in fear |
| RAPTURE | Delight; joy |
| RETALIATION | Revenge; getting even |
| SAGACITY | Wisdom |
| SCANTY | Less than is needed |

| SCATHING | Scornful; mocking |
| --- | --- |
| SUNDERED | Separated |
| VIGILANCE | Care; watchfulness |
| VINDICATION | Support; justification |

## Frederick Douglass Vocabulary

| DETESTATION | INCOHERENT | SAGACITY | IMBIBED | AGITATED |
|---|---|---|---|---|
| CONSUMMATE | CENSURED | EXCULPATE | COMMENSURATE | MYRIADS |
| IMPUTATIONS | IMPUDENCE | FREE SPACE | AUTHENTIC | SCANTY |
| BENEVOLENCE | EMANCIPATION | DEPRAVITY | DESTITUTE | CONJECTURE |
| IMPERTINENT | PERPLEXING | PROVIDENCE | MAXIM | DEFICIENCY |

## Frederick Douglass Vocabulary

| VINDICATION | ARDENTLY | OBDURATE | VIGILANCE | AVAILED |
|---|---|---|---|---|
| ODIOUSNESS | IMBUE | SUNDERED | DENUNCIATION | MANIFESTATION |
| PERNICIOUS | PERDITION | FREE SPACE | APPALLED | RAPTURE |
| PROFLIGATE | DEFILED | DESOLATE | IMMUTABLE | ABHORRENCE |
| EXHORTED | INFIDEL | SCATHING | RETALIATION | DEFICIENCY |

## Frederick Douglass Vocabulary

| DEFICIENCY | ARDENTLY | ANNIHILATE | BENEVOLENCE | VIGILANCE |
|---|---|---|---|---|
| PROVIDENCE | APPALLED | SAGACITY | MAXIM | PERDITION |
| IMMUTABLE | RETALIATION | FREE SPACE | COMMENSURATE | IMPERTINENT |
| AVAILED | IMPUDENCE | SUNDERED | VINDICATION | PERNICIOUS |
| SCATHING | PERPLEXING | CONJECTURE | PROFLIGATE | DENUNCIATION |

## Frederick Douglass Vocabulary

| DEFILED | INCOHERENT | DETESTATION | MANIFESTATION | ABHORRENCE |
|---|---|---|---|---|
| CONSUMMATE | OBDURATE | AUTHENTIC | EMANCIPATION | QUAILED |
| CENSURED | IMPUTATIONS | FREE SPACE | EXHORTED | DEPRAVITY |
| DESTITUTE | MYRIADS | AGITATED | IMBIBED | SCANTY |
| RAPTURE | DESOLATE | EXCULPATE | IMBUE | DENUNCIATION |

Frederick Douglass Vocabulary

| SUNDERED | VINDICATION | DEFICIENCY | CENSURED | BENEVOLENCE |
|---|---|---|---|---|
| MANIFESTATION | PERDITION | PROVIDENCE | APPALLED | IMPERTINENT |
| RAPTURE | DESOLATE | FREE SPACE | SCATHING | QUAILED |
| DEFILED | MYRIADS | ODIOUSNESS | ABHORRENCE | INFIDEL |
| DEPRAVITY | CONJECTURE | IMBUE | AVAILED | PERNICIOUS |

Frederick Douglass Vocabulary

| AUTHENTIC | CONSUMMATE | IMPUTATIONS | ARDENTLY | IMBIBED |
|---|---|---|---|---|
| INCOHERENT | DESTITUTE | AGITATED | PROFLIGATE | EXHORTED |
| DENUNCIATION | IMPUDENCE | FREE SPACE | SAGACITY | EXCULPATE |
| DETESTATION | VIGILANCE | SCANTY | EMANCIPATION | COMMENSURATE |
| OBDURATE | RETALIATION | MAXIM | PERPLEXING | PERNICIOUS |

## Frederick Douglass Vocabulary

| ARDENTLY | APPALLED | RAPTURE | DEFILED | SAGACITY |
|---|---|---|---|---|
| DEFICIENCY | DEPRAVITY | EXHORTED | RETALIATION | BENEVOLENCE |
| MYRIADS | VIGILANCE | FREE SPACE | PERNICIOUS | IMPUTATIONS |
| DENUNCIATION | EMANCIPATION | DESOLATE | ABHORRENCE | AGITATED |
| DESTITUTE | AUTHENTIC | QUAILED | DETESTATION | IMPUDENCE |

## Frederick Douglass Vocabulary

| VINDICATION | SUNDERED | PERDITION | COMMENSURATE | IMMUTABLE |
|---|---|---|---|---|
| PROVIDENCE | INFIDEL | SCANTY | CONSUMMATE | IMPERTINENT |
| EXCULPATE | IMBIBED | FREE SPACE | ANNIHILATE | CONJECTURE |
| PERPLEXING | MAXIM | PROFLIGATE | SCATHING | CENSURED |
| IMBUE | INCOHERENT | MANIFESTATION | ODIOUSNESS | IMPUDENCE |

## Frederick Douglass Vocabulary

| VIGILANCE | IMBIBED | AVAILED | INFIDEL | CONJECTURE |
|---|---|---|---|---|
| VINDICATION | DESOLATE | IMPUDENCE | SCANTY | PROFLIGATE |
| EXCULPATE | DEFILED | FREE SPACE | INCOHERENT | EMANCIPATION |
| DEPRAVITY | COMMENSURATE | PERNICIOUS | ABHORRENCE | RAPTURE |
| APPALLED | RETALIATION | DESTITUTE | OBDURATE | IMPERTINENT |

## Frederick Douglass Vocabulary

| SAGACITY | PERPLEXING | EXHORTED | IMMUTABLE | IMPUTATIONS |
|---|---|---|---|---|
| DENUNCIATION | CENSURED | IMBUE | AGITATED | MAXIM |
| SUNDERED | SCATHING | FREE SPACE | MANIFESTATION | DEFICIENCY |
| ODIOUSNESS | PROVIDENCE | MYRIADS | QUAILED | ARDENTLY |
| CONSUMMATE | DETESTATION | PERDITION | BENEVOLENCE | IMPERTINENT |

## Frederick Douglass Vocabulary

| EXCULPATE | SAGACITY | IMPUDENCE | AVAILED | MYRIADS |
|---|---|---|---|---|
| AUTHENTIC | CONSUMMATE | BENEVOLENCE | PERPLEXING | EMANCIPATION |
| DEFILED | PROVIDENCE | FREE SPACE | DEFICIENCY | ODIOUSNESS |
| DESOLATE | PERDITION | ABHORRENCE | APPALLED | INFIDEL |
| EXHORTED | RETALIATION | IMBUE | ARDENTLY | IMMUTABLE |

## Frederick Douglass Vocabulary

| DESTITUTE | IMPERTINENT | DEPRAVITY | MAXIM | SCANTY |
|---|---|---|---|---|
| SCATHING | PROFLIGATE | OBDURATE | CONJECTURE | VINDICATION |
| CENSURED | VIGILANCE | FREE SPACE | COMMENSURATE | INCOHERENT |
| SUNDERED | DETESTATION | AGITATED | MANIFESTATION | QUAILED |
| IMBIBED | PERNICIOUS | IMPUTATIONS | RAPTURE | IMMUTABLE |

## Frederick Douglass Vocabulary

| VIGILANCE | QUAILED | IMMUTABLE | PROFLIGATE | AUTHENTIC |
|---|---|---|---|---|
| ODIOUSNESS | MAXIM | CENSURED | INCOHERENT | PERPLEXING |
| IMPERTINENT | ARDENTLY | FREE SPACE | ANNIHILATE | DEFILED |
| DESTITUTE | RETALIATION | DEFICIENCY | EXCULPATE | ABHORRENCE |
| CONJECTURE | APPALLED | PERDITION | EMANCIPATION | SAGACITY |

## Frederick Douglass Vocabulary

| PROVIDENCE | SUNDERED | OBDURATE | COMMENSURATE | BENEVOLENCE |
|---|---|---|---|---|
| SCATHING | DESOLATE | IMBIBED | INFIDEL | EXHORTED |
| SCANTY | IMBUE | FREE SPACE | DETESTATION | CONSUMMATE |
| VINDICATION | DEPRAVITY | DENUNCIATION | AVAILED | MANIFESTATION |
| AGITATED | RAPTURE | IMPUTATIONS | PERNICIOUS | SAGACITY |

## Frederick Douglass Vocabulary

| DETESTATION | CONSUMMATE | IMMUTABLE | SCATHING | CONJECTURE |
|---|---|---|---|---|
| BENEVOLENCE | IMPUDENCE | AVAILED | SUNDERED | ANNIHILATE |
| EXHORTED | MYRIADS | FREE SPACE | ARDENTLY | MANIFESTATION |
| PROFLIGATE | RAPTURE | IMBIBED | COMMENSURATE | AUTHENTIC |
| DENUNCIATION | PERPLEXING | PERNICIOUS | DESTITUTE | DEFICIENCY |

## Frederick Douglass Vocabulary

| DESOLATE | QUAILED | EXCULPATE | EMANCIPATION | VINDICATION |
|---|---|---|---|---|
| SAGACITY | SCANTY | DEPRAVITY | AGITATED | MAXIM |
| DEFILED | INFIDEL | FREE SPACE | APPALLED | CENSURED |
| RETALIATION | PERDITION | ODIOUSNESS | ABHORRENCE | PROVIDENCE |
| IMPERTINENT | IMPUTATIONS | INCOHERENT | IMBUE | DEFICIENCY |

## Frederick Douglass Vocabulary

| SAGACITY | EMANCIPATION | CONJECTURE | DEFICIENCY | IMMUTABLE |
|---|---|---|---|---|
| IMBIBED | AUTHENTIC | EXHORTED | INFIDEL | APPALLED |
| IMBUE | DENUNCIATION | FREE SPACE | QUAILED | PROVIDENCE |
| VIGILANCE | COMMENSURATE | MYRIADS | DEFILED | IMPUTATIONS |
| AGITATED | ABHORRENCE | CENSURED | IMPUDENCE | OBDURATE |

## Frederick Douglass Vocabulary

| SUNDERED | RETALIATION | DEPRAVITY | EXCULPATE | DESOLATE |
|---|---|---|---|---|
| PERDITION | ANNIHILATE | SCANTY | ODIOUSNESS | INCOHERENT |
| SCATHING | DETESTATION | FREE SPACE | PERNICIOUS | BENEVOLENCE |
| MAXIM | PERPLEXING | AVAILED | IMPERTINENT | ARDENTLY |
| VINDICATION | CONSUMMATE | RAPTURE | PROFLIGATE | OBDURATE |

## Frederick Douglass Vocabulary

| CONSUMMATE | IMMUTABLE | EXHORTED | BENEVOLENCE | MYRIADS |
|---|---|---|---|---|
| ANNIHILATE | IMBIBED | MANIFESTATION | EXCULPATE | IMPERTINENT |
| SUNDERED | DESOLATE | FREE SPACE | CONJECTURE | INFIDEL |
| CENSURED | RETALIATION | OBDURATE | SCANTY | DEPRAVITY |
| AGITATED | PROVIDENCE | VINDICATION | PERPLEXING | IMBUE |

## Frederick Douglass Vocabulary

| VIGILANCE | DESTITUTE | RAPTURE | MAXIM | QUAILED |
|---|---|---|---|---|
| DEFICIENCY | SCATHING | ARDENTLY | DENUNCIATION | DETESTATION |
| INCOHERENT | AVAILED | FREE SPACE | PROFLIGATE | DEFILED |
| PERNICIOUS | EMANCIPATION | APPALLED | SAGACITY | PERDITION |
| ODIOUSNESS | IMPUTATIONS | IMPUDENCE | ABHORRENCE | IMBUE |

## Frederick Douglass Vocabulary

| AVAILED | ABHORRENCE | EXHORTED | VIGILANCE | VINDICATION |
|---|---|---|---|---|
| IMPUTATIONS | INFIDEL | ODIOUSNESS | IMBUE | DEPRAVITY |
| QUAILED | MANIFESTATION | FREE SPACE | OBDURATE | IMPERTINENT |
| AGITATED | DEFILED | DESTITUTE | EMANCIPATION | SUNDERED |
| BENEVOLENCE | SCANTY | IMPUDENCE | AUTHENTIC | IMBIBED |

## Frederick Douglass Vocabulary

| ARDENTLY | CONSUMMATE | DESOLATE | ANNIHILATE | CENSURED |
|---|---|---|---|---|
| SAGACITY | SCATHING | IMMUTABLE | MAXIM | CONJECTURE |
| PERDITION | EXCULPATE | FREE SPACE | DENUNCIATION | RAPTURE |
| DETESTATION | APPALLED | MYRIADS | PERNICIOUS | PROFLIGATE |
| PERPLEXING | INCOHERENT | PROVIDENCE | RETALIATION | IMBIBED |

## Frederick Douglass Vocabulary

| IMBUE | EXHORTED | PERNICIOUS | IMPUTATIONS | CONJECTURE |
|---|---|---|---|---|
| CENSURED | APPALLED | EXCULPATE | ANNIHILATE | OBDURATE |
| ODIOUSNESS | IMPUDENCE | FREE SPACE | AVAILED | AGITATED |
| PROVIDENCE | DETESTATION | DESOLATE | DEFILED | EMANCIPATION |
| PERDITION | MAXIM | INFIDEL | DEPRAVITY | DEFICIENCY |

## Frederick Douglass Vocabulary

| SCATHING | MYRIADS | IMMUTABLE | RETALIATION | CONSUMMATE |
|---|---|---|---|---|
| VINDICATION | BENEVOLENCE | ABHORRENCE | MANIFESTATION | ARDENTLY |
| SAGACITY | AUTHENTIC | FREE SPACE | RAPTURE | COMMENSURATE |
| DENUNCIATION | DESTITUTE | VIGILANCE | SUNDERED | PERPLEXING |
| SCANTY | IMPERTINENT | PROFLIGATE | INCOHERENT | DEFICIENCY |

## Frederick Douglass Vocabulary

| AGITATED | IMMUTABLE | ABHORRENCE | DEFICIENCY | OBDURATE |
|---|---|---|---|---|
| DEPRAVITY | CONSUMMATE | IMPUDENCE | BENEVOLENCE | SUNDERED |
| EXHORTED | MAXIM | FREE SPACE | SAGACITY | IMPUTATIONS |
| PERNICIOUS | RAPTURE | QUAILED | DEFILED | DESOLATE |
| RETALIATION | VIGILANCE | INFIDEL | DETESTATION | PROFLIGATE |

## Frederick Douglass Vocabulary

| EMANCIPATION | ODIOUSNESS | ARDENTLY | IMBIBED | SCANTY |
|---|---|---|---|---|
| INCOHERENT | EXCULPATE | CONJECTURE | DENUNCIATION | IMPERTINENT |
| PERDITION | SCATHING | FREE SPACE | MANIFESTATION | AVAILED |
| CENSURED | ANNIHILATE | PERPLEXING | PROVIDENCE | AUTHENTIC |
| APPALLED | VINDICATION | DESTITUTE | MYRIADS | PROFLIGATE |

Frederick Douglass Vocabulary

| PROVIDENCE | IMPUDENCE | AGITATED | EXHORTED | AUTHENTIC |
|---|---|---|---|---|
| EXCULPATE | DEFICIENCY | DEPRAVITY | ARDENTLY | CONSUMMATE |
| APPALLED | IMPERTINENT | FREE SPACE | MAXIM | VIGILANCE |
| CONJECTURE | SUNDERED | BENEVOLENCE | CENSURED | OBDURATE |
| DESOLATE | MANIFESTATION | DENUNCIATION | PERNICIOUS | IMBUE |

Frederick Douglass Vocabulary

| AVAILED | IMPUTATIONS | PERPLEXING | ODIOUSNESS | SCATHING |
|---|---|---|---|---|
| PERDITION | RETALIATION | QUAILED | IMBIBED | DESTITUTE |
| SCANTY | DETESTATION | FREE SPACE | ABHORRENCE | INCOHERENT |
| PROFLIGATE | INFIDEL | EMANCIPATION | DEFILED | VINDICATION |
| ANNIHILATE | IMMUTABLE | RAPTURE | SAGACITY | IMBUE |

## Frederick Douglass Vocabulary

| VINDICATION | IMPERTINENT | ODIOUSNESS | INCOHERENT | QUAILED |
|---|---|---|---|---|
| MAXIM | CONSUMMATE | PROFLIGATE | INFIDEL | IMBIBED |
| RAPTURE | VIGILANCE | FREE SPACE | DEPRAVITY | IMMUTABLE |
| MANIFESTATION | PERPLEXING | SCATHING | AGITATED | MYRIADS |
| ANNIHILATE | DEFICIENCY | EMANCIPATION | DESTITUTE | RETALIATION |

## Frederick Douglass Vocabulary

| IMBUE | OBDURATE | CONJECTURE | DENUNCIATION | AUTHENTIC |
|---|---|---|---|---|
| SAGACITY | ABHORRENCE | APPALLED | AVAILED | CENSURED |
| COMMENSURATE | EXHORTED | FREE SPACE | IMPUTATIONS | EXCULPATE |
| ARDENTLY | SUNDERED | PERNICIOUS | PROVIDENCE | SCANTY |
| IMPUDENCE | DETESTATION | PERDITION | DEFILED | RETALIATION |

## Frederick Douglass Vocabulary

| PERDITION | CENSURED | DEPRAVITY | PERNICIOUS | MANIFESTATION |
|---|---|---|---|---|
| VIGILANCE | AUTHENTIC | DETESTATION | SCATHING | EXHORTED |
| INCOHERENT | IMMUTABLE | FREE SPACE | IMPERTINENT | VINDICATION |
| COMMENSURATE | IMPUTATIONS | SAGACITY | ODIOUSNESS | IMBUE |
| PROFLIGATE | SUNDERED | DESTITUTE | DESOLATE | IMBIBED |

## Frederick Douglass Vocabulary

| EXCULPATE | RETALIATION | AGITATED | ANNIHILATE | EMANCIPATION |
|---|---|---|---|---|
| SCANTY | PERPLEXING | OBDURATE | CONSUMMATE | DEFILED |
| DEFICIENCY | INFIDEL | FREE SPACE | BENEVOLENCE | RAPTURE |
| IMPUDENCE | QUAILED | MYRIADS | AVAILED | APPALLED |
| ARDENTLY | CONJECTURE | PROVIDENCE | DENUNCIATION | IMBIBED |

www.ingramcontent.com/pod-product-compliance
Lightning Source LLC
Chambersburg PA
CBHW081456070526
44586CB00019B/2374